T]

Awakened Parent Challenge

by Darren Curtis

How to strengthen the connection with your teenager in 7 days

"This is a long overdue book – it's a brilliant masterpiece that should be in the hands of every adult, parent, teacher, counsellor and the youth themselves."
– Kathy Buckley

British Library Cataloguing in Publication Data
A record for this book is available from the British Library.

ISBN-Paperback: 978-0-9574604-1-6
ISBN-eBook: 978-0-9574604-2-3

Typeset by SWATT Books Ltd., Southampton.

Printed and bound in Great Britain

Absolutely Fabulous Ltd
25 Westwood Road,
Reading, RG31 5PL

Welcome to The Awakened Parent Challenge

Fellow Parent,

You and I know how frustrated, overwhelmed and unappreciated we can feel when our little bundles of joy explode into their teenage years.

Having navigated my own children through their teenage years, and with over 18 years' experience as an international youth coach in schools, colleges and youth leadership events, I've discovered simple solutions to the areas which are currently causing you arguments, worry and guilt.

In as little as 7 days, if you choose to take The Awakened Parent Challenge, the solutions I share will completely and permanently improve your relationship with your teen or pre-teen beyond anything you could currently imagine.

Read and enjoy!

*Children who challenge us
the most are our
best teachers.*

Unknown

Foreword

"Darren gives you the tools to get to the core of understanding, communicating and honouring our youth, to help gain their self-respect, self-confidence and significance in a positive way; simply by listening and choosing your words wisely. He will show you how to have the compassion and patience to develop a long-lasting, healthy relationship with your growing and changing youth.

This is a long overdue book, it's a brilliant masterpiece that should be in the hands of every adult, parent, teacher, counsellor and the youth themselves. It's a must-read. I work with youth from all over the world, why didn't I think of this!

You rock Mr Curtis!"

Kathy Buckley
Actress, Comedian, Motivational Speaker

Dreams come with built-in challenges; challenges come with built-in dreams.

Mike Dooley

Acknowledgements

It seems hard to believe that I started scribbling my thoughts, observations and stories onto paper some twelve years ago this very week whilst working in San Diego, so it seems fitting that I am writing the final part of this book in San Diego whilst on vacation.

The easiest and most obvious thank you is to my wife Tracy,

I am so grateful for the time, space and support given to me since I embarked on writing this book. When I have been away, writing, she has taken care of things back home, allowing me to relax and get creative. She's been supportive and above all, believed in me and what I am trying to achieve. To my darling wife, thank you, thank you, thank you.

A huge thank you must go to my boys, Danny and Bailey – you are my inspiration, thank you for keeping me grounded and feeling younger than the birthdate printed on my passport would have you believe. I am so proud of you both for simply being yourselves.

Thank you to my brother Colin for letting me use his home in the Highlands of Scotland when I needed to get away to gather my thoughts and for spending the time to read through and constructively comment on the chapters.

Thank you to my Mum and Dad for loving me unconditionally throughout my childhood and helping me to grow into a happy, confident adult. Thanks to my dad for helping me to always remember "you gotta have a laugh boy", a truly wonderful voice to have inside my head, thank you, thank you, thank you.

Thank you to my sisters, Jackie and Cindy, for always being there. Your sisterly love is very much appreciated, I love you both very much, thank you, thank you, thank you.

Thank you to all my teachers who made learning fun and interesting and a special thank you to the teachers who made me feel like an idiot (and I mean that most sincerely) because without you, I wouldn't have such a strong desire to help teenagers as I do today and this book would not have been written, so thank you, thank you, thank you.

Many, many thanks go to all the team, speakers, coaches, youth coaches and anyone who has ever attended the Anthony Robbins Foundation global youth leadership summit (too numerous to mention, but you know who you all are). Your energy and commitment are inspiring, I learn much more than I can ever teach whenever I spend time with you all, thank you, thank you, thank you.

Thank you so much to Davina Rasmussen, my first life coach, who opened my eyes to a completely new way of thinking and being. Your presence in my life all those years ago has had a profound effect on the direction of not only my life, but that of my wife's, my children and everyone I have gone on to work with. You are truly a spark that lit a flame within me, thank you, thank you, thank you. Also, thank you Davina for introducing me to Anthony Robbins, for it is a combination of what you and Tony initially taught me which has formed the foundation of the book you hold in your hands. Thank you, Tony for all that you have done and continue to do, you are a very special man.

Thank you to Mark Beaumont-Thomas at Lexicon Marketing for your help with editing and Sam Pearce from SWATT Books for your help with typesetting and artwork for the second edition, Thank you, Thank you, Thank you.

Thank you to Heather Miller for helping create more clarity for parents around social media usage and cyber-bullying. Thank you, thank you, thank you.

And no thanks would be complete without thanking two very special people, Richard Wilkins and Liz Ivory for their fabulous Broadband Consciousness course and their analogy of the script versus conscious choosing, which was the missing piece of the puzzle for me.

Finally, thank you to you the reader for having enough faith in me as an author to read this book from beginning to end and to start to make the tiny changes necessary in your life to become more connected with yourself and your loved ones. I honour you, thank you, thank you, thank you.

Darren Curtis

> *When you replace the words always and never with the word sometimes, it's so much easier to stay calm.*
>
> Darren Curtis

Important

This book is not intended as a substitute for the medical advice of physicians. You should consult a physician in matters relating to yours or your child's health and particularly with respect to any symptoms that may require diagnosis or medical attention.

Why me, why now?

Why me, why now?
Because I care and the time is right.

When I was 5 years old, my mother always told me that happiness was the key to life. When I went to school, they asked me what I wanted to be when I grew up. I wrote down 'happy'. They told me I didn't understand the assignment, and I told them they didn't understand life.

John Lennon

To say I wasn't the most academic kid in school is a gross understatement.

I guess I'm so passionate about the subject of teenagers and how to communicate more effectively with them because I believe they are so often dismissed, undermined, and misunderstood through no fault of their own. I'm aware that my last statement flies in the face of common thinking, but hey, following the herd was never really my thing and the following story may well give you a flavour of where my passion comes from.

I remember being in what is now referred to as Year 7 at school, when my English teacher asked me to stand up in front of the class and read from my book aloud. I was a reluctant reader, with a belief back then that reading was boring (more about the effects of your beliefs later in the book). I don't know about you but reading from a book in front of my classmates was one of my least favourite things to do.

2

After spending what seemed like a lifetime Er! Ah! and Um-ing! my way through the sentences, I had barely completed a paragraph. The teacher stopped me abruptly and with an undertone of sheer disappointment bellowed, "That was awful Darren. My seven –year-old daughter could do better than that. Sit down." I remember sitting down as fast as I could, my cheeks burning bright red with embarrassment, thinking what a cow she was to embarrass me in front of my friends.

I can now sit here as an adult and ask myself, what possible good can my teacher have expected by speaking to one of her students like that? I didn't realise it at the time, but when I look back I can see that I was one of the lucky ones, because my parents had let me know from as far back as I can remember, I could do anything I put my mind to and I was loved for being me, not for the grades I achieved.

From this I developed a supportive internal voice which says, "It's OK, I'm OK and it'll be OK". So, although this teacher's comments did affect me with regard to crushing my desire to read even further (especially out loud!), it didn't affect who I was as a person. But I know, from working with thousands of teenagers over the years, that most of them do not have that supportive internal voice or a parent who thinks they're the greatest thing since sliced bread. They are usually full of doubt and negativity, with a parent or teacher's voice in their head which says, "Who do you think you are?" "You'll never amount to anything", "You're as thick as two short planks", "I'm disappointed in you" or much, much worse.

I was talking to a highly articulate homeless guy on the streets of San Diego whilst writing some of the chapters for this book. He shared with me that he could still hear his late father's voice shouting at him, "You're a bum, you'll always be a bum!" Do you see the irony there? I'm sure his father didn't want or intend for his son to literally become a "bum", but your words as parents and teachers have the

3

power to shape a youngster's decisions about what choices they make, what they choose to do or, just as importantly, what not to do, the relationships they enter into and their relative fulfilment in life. So, no pressure there then, eh!

In my eighth year at school, I had escaped from my previous English teacher, only to be saddled with an equally venomous replacement (I'm sure she was a wonderful lady out of school – lol!) When she was absent from school one week, we were asked by our stand-in teacher to write a poem about war or destruction. This was my first experience of writing poetry and I thoroughly enjoyed it. We were asked to finish off the poem for homework and hand it in to our usual English teacher at the following lesson. I proudly handed in my poem, knowing I had produced something quite special, only to be met with the words, "Are you sure this is your own work Darren, it seems far too good for you?" There's nothing like a bit of encouragement is there?

Those examples are from my schooling in the late 1970s/early 80s and obviously things have come along considerably since then, haven't they? Well in some ways yes, but my own son went through a period with a teacher who seemed to have little emotional intelligence. When he was in primary school, she would call him to the front of the class and shout, "Bailey, you are irresponsible!" Surely he had misheard her, surely a teacher wouldn't attack an eight year old's entire identity, would they?

Nowadays every teacher is taught the importance of disciplining a child's behaviour rather than their identity. If you are not already aware of the importance of this fact, more will be revealed as you continue reading. However, it would seem that some teachers still ignore that vital piece of learning and continue to implant a damaging negative inner voice into a child's head. Luckily, my son knew this was wrong, which is why he brought it to my attention. He admitted what he'd done was probably irresponsible, but thankfully he knows that he is not an irresponsible child, because he has grown up hearing his mother and I talking about the psychology behind identity versus behaviour. More about this in Chapter Eight.

If you are a parent whose child is coming up to or is already a pre-teen or teenager, then this book is written especially for you. Because I know that a lot of what you are currently doing isn't working for you or your child and this is causing you and them some major stress. My original idea was to write something for my own teenage boys to assist their journeys into adulthood, but on chatting to them they seem OK with most things. So, I got to thinking about all the other parents I see who are stressed and struggling through their child's pre-teen and teenage years, most of which seems totally unnecessary. So, this book has been written to piece together all the little gems which I've discovered through working with secondary/high school aged youth around the globe. It is an attempt to simplify and share the tools, techniques and actions necessary to create or recreate an effective communication channel between you and your children.

I'm also aware of how frustrating it can be for teachers of older children and I truly admire some of the work you do. However, I have to say, some teachers I've met and experienced really don't do themselves many favours. You probably know one or two? Maybe you could politely suggest they read this book? If you are a teacher whose colleague has politely suggested you read this book, welcome, and enjoy the ride. You're gonna love it. Apologies in advance to any English teachers – I've probably made the odd punctuation and grammatical error and to be honest I'm actually not that fussed, because this book is about helping you to make tiny shifts in your psychology to help you, and the children you interact with. It's not about being grammatically correct.

I also think the time is right to change the age-old perception that somehow most teenagers are monsters. We can learn just as much from our teenagers as we can ever hope to teach them. The trick is to shut up and listen sometimes, something we preach to our children, but often conveniently forget to do ourselves.

Every day I hear parents who are constantly moaning about their children, especially their teen or pre-teen. But I'm also aware, even with all the knowledge my wife and I have accumulated in this field, how wrong we sometimes get it when we are tired, hungry or under pressure and emotions are running high. I suspect you often feel the same. You get so annoyed and frustrated that you can't communicate without shouting at your youngster and then you beat yourself up for not handling it well or for losing control in the most spectacular fashion.

Well, before we go any further, I'd like to introduce you to the concept of "the script". This is a reference to that inner critic, the negative voice in your head that judges you and tells you that you're not a good parent or that you're getting things wrong, or even that you're a bad person. Two of my own mentors, Richard Wilkins and Liz Ivory, teach the analogy that the script is just your conditioning, handed down by parents, teachers and society. It is a list of experiences you've had that have caused a negative feeling. It recalls how you felt when you got it wrong, embarrassed yourself, got hurt, felt different, weren't good enough, failed, felt lonely or anxious and anything else that made you feel bad. The script is there as a reminder of what not to do. It is there to try to keep you safe. It will constantly criticise you, compare you unfavourably to others and look out for anything that may cause you to fail and experience those bad feelings again.

When you become aware of the script and its constant judgement, you can choose to see it for what it is: a basic, primitive survival mode that will only ever focus on fear. Then you can choose to separate from it and speak to yourself with supportive, kind and positive words. That may sound too simple, (at least that's what your script will tell you), but what would you choose? Would you choose to feel good about yourself or would you choose to feel bad? Obviously, if you could choose, you'd always choose to feel good. So that must mean that when you feel bad, which as a human being you sometimes do, it simply means that it is not you who is choosing. It is the script.

Learning about the script and knowing that the negative internal voice, (the audio version of the script), is not Me, has helped me enormously in all my relationships.

This book is intended to be an aid for parents and teachers to help them to stop listening to the script, its judgements, and its criticism. Instead, it will help you to start to choose how you really want to communicate and connect with the youngsters in your life.

This will not only help you to get more of what you want out of life, it will also ensure that you are happy with who you are and with the choices you make. It will add to the enrichment of ALL your relationships. After all, isn't that what we all want for ourselves and our children?

The illiterate of the 21st century will not be those who cannot read and write, but those who cannot learn, unlearn, and relearn.

Alwin Toffler

take the
challenge

Take the 7-day
Awakened Parent Challenge!

Take the 7-day Awakened Parent Challenge!

If you're up for it, in the space of just one week, you can complete The Awakened Parent Challenge as you read along with this book. For this Challenge, let's assume that your week is going to start on a Monday. We have drawn up a schedule which starts on Monday morning and is completed by the Sunday evening. Of course, you can choose to start on any day of the week which suits you, but Monday morning is a logical moment to get going!

Here is a summary of the challenges and solutions which each chapter gives you. Refer to this as a quick checklist at the end of your seven days, to check that you have successfully completed it!

MONDAY

Chapter One: Mind your language
Perfecting the art of asking what you want your teenager to do, instead of what you DON'T want!

Chapter Two: Worrying about an if
How to steer teenagers away from fearing the worst to imagining that the best can happen.

TUESDAY

Chapter Three: Motivation
How to move from being a problem-solver to becoming a solution-seeker: it makes a world of difference!

Chapter Four: What's important to you?
Understanding the important distinction between what is important to you and what matters to your teenager.

WEDNESDAY

Chapter Five: Changing your internal voice – as simple as ABC
Showing the vital difference between Script FM and Friend FM in everyone's choice of internal radio stations.

Chapter Six: Is it true or not?
Understanding the power of the subconscious mind and the value of focusing on solutions instead of problems.

THURSDAY

Chapter Seven: Pain and pleasure are the catalyst for change
Being aware of this simple basis for all our actions makes all the difference + some useful guidelines on bullying and smartphone use.

Chapter Eight: Praise their identity, discipline their behaviour
Illustrating this vital distinction in the way we can talk to our teenagers to achieve instant and longer term results.

FRIDAY

Chapter Nine: Winning the game
A recognition of the value of different types of intelligence.

Chapter Ten: Pick your battles
If you want more peace and harmony in your household, then this is a vital skill to understand and practice.

SATURDAY

Chapter Eleven: Listening
Most of us have no idea how to listen – why? Because we've never been taught. In this chapter, you'll learn the three levels of listening and how to use them to your advantage.

Chapter Twelve: Perception is reality
The power of encouragement and support. The clever use of visualisation and the power of a positively framed question.

SUNDAY

Chapter Thirteen: Eat, drink and be happy...
The critical importance of the right sort of diet.

Chapter Fourteen: Keep calm and carry on
Making solid ongoing commitments which will cement the progress made during this Challenge.

Once you've completed the Challenge

So, there you go, fourteen important aspects of successfully parenting a teenager, all covered in just seven days. To help The Awakened Parent Challenge be more than just agreeing (hopefully!) with the proven advice, tips and techniques shared in this book, at the end of most chapters are sections for you to write down actions which YOU commit to on an ongoing basis. This book is designed to be interactive, full of YOUR notes, thoughts, and future commitments. On that basis, keep referring to it in the weeks and months ahead. Alternatively, you can take the Challenge online at www.darrencurtis.com/challenge. Good luck!

Chapter

Mind your language

Mind your language

Why is it whenever most people see a sign that says, "Wet paint, do not touch", they need to go and touch it? Or at least get the urge to touch it, just to check. It's the same wall or door frame they have walked past without touching for many years, but as soon as the sign instructs them "do not touch", they feel compelled to touch it.

Most parents and teachers I speak to know what they don't want. They don't want their kids to be naughty, they don't want them to be disrespectful, they don't want them to get in with the wrong crowd and they don't want them to be late for class or to come home late.

Unfortunately, our subconscious mind doesn't recognise the difference between a positive or a negative instruction. Let me share some interesting facts which will help to clarify this.

We are all susceptible to others' suggestions. When you communicate with your children you are attempting to persuade them to do certain things in certain ways. When you watch a television advert, the company is trying to persuade you to choose their product over their competitors'. Hypnosis is based on the power of suggestion and as a certified hypnotist I can assure you that it's just as easy for someone to hypnotise themselves or others about what they don't want as it is to hypnotise them regarding what they do want.

Not sure what I'm talking about? Try this exercise. Whatever happens, please do not think of a pink cat. Just to be crystal clear, you can think about anything except a pink cat.

Are you thinking of a pink cat when I specifically asked you not to?

In fact, you have probably never thought of a pink cat until the moment I asked you not to think of one. Unless of course you're a big fan of *Bagpuss* and I've just brought back childhood memories of that wonderful BBC children's series, or maybe it has conjured up images of the Cheshire cat from *Alice in Wonderland*. I must confess to being a fan of both.

Even if you say you weren't thinking of a pink cat consciously, your subconscious mind had to create a picture of one for you to know what I was asking you not to think of. How strange is that? Bizarrely enough, you may now even think of a pink cat before you go to bed tonight or dream about one, just because I asked you not to think of one. That is just a small demonstration of the power of language to direct our focus or that of our children's where we least want it to go.

So, might you be guilty of telling your children to focus on exactly what you don't want?

"Don't answer back!"
"Don't speak to me like that!"
"Don't be home late!"
"Don't be so disrespectful!"

"Don't leave your homework until the last minute!"
"Don't forget your keys!"

Are these things you might say in an attempt to gain control of a situation?

Or is your script, your inner critic, telling you that you've been too soft, dealt with things in the wrong way and that you need to be firmer?

May I be so bold as to ask you, how well is that working for you? Not so good, I would guess, because this is your equivalent of the big pink cat!!!

Let's just remove the word "don't" from all those commands and see what you're actually programming or hypnotising them to do.

"Answer back"
"Speak to me like that"
"Be home late"
"Be so disrespectful"
"Leave your homework until the last minute"
"Forget your keys"

Exactly what you don't want!!! Crazy, but true. I'm sure you can add another dozen well-used negative requests/phrases to the list which you regularly bark at your children.

Examples of more positive ways to request what you want would be:

"I need you to listen"
"Please speak to me with some respect"
"Please be home on time" or "Please be home before 9pm"
"Please do your homework on time"
"Please remember your keys"

one

You may be reading this book because you have a problem or challenges with your child. My question to you is: "What exactly do you want from your child?"

I know you may think you don't know what you want, because like many other parents and teachers I work with, you're stuck in a rut and find yourself saying the same things over and over again, getting the same result or lack of results. I call this the *'fly at the window'* syndrome.

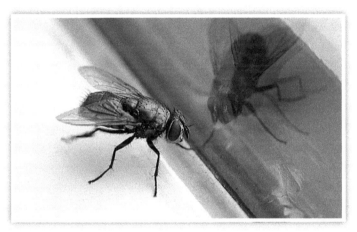

Have you ever seen a fly bouncing off the windowpane?

What does the fly want? It wants to find a way out, freedom, right? But it keeps hitting the same windowpane over and over again. And no matter how many times the fly does this, each time it expects a different result and we all know that ain't gonna happen. So, you either squash him or if you're like me, you open the nearest window to let him out.

But what does the little fella do? Does he take the hint and fly straight out the open window or does he usually carry on bouncing off the same windowpane, even though the escape route is only centimetres away? Even when I gently encourage him in the general direction of the open window to freedom, he still keeps banging his head against the same windowpane, expecting a different result.

Well the good news is, the solution to your problem or challenge is closer than you think. You just need to choose to stop banging your head against the same windowpane.

Here are two stories which demonstrate the power of the subconscious programming you and I do all the time, and how we get what we don't ask for (i.e. we instead get what we ask for in a negative way).

For some reason best known to the carpet cleaning pixies, the majority of drinks I would give to my children when they were young would be spilt, despite my continuous requests for them to "Please don't spill it". I was painfully aware that what I was doing wasn't working. Something had to change and so my experiment commenced.

I handed them each a plastic cup half-filled with juice, telling them "Please don't spill it", stepped back and watched them without their knowledge. They would take a sip, then place the half-full cups on the carpet next to where they were playing. Six minutes and 37 seconds later Danny swung his leg round and over the cup went. Imagine, as suggested earlier, taking the word "don't" out of the instruction. I was basically giving them the request or suggestion to "please spill the drink" and they duly obliged.

What was it I really wanted them to do? I wanted them to be careful. So, I changed my strategy and asked them, *"Please be careful with your drink"* as I handed the drinks to them later the same day. Now I'd told them what I wanted, I once again stepped back and observed them without their knowledge. To my surprise, I watched them place the cup of juice on the small table next to the sofa, play for a while, take a slurp, go back to play and repeat this until the drink was all gone, this time into their bellies rather than onto the carpet! Just to be sure this wasn't a fluke, I reverted to my old negatively framed request of "Don't spill your drink" and more often than not it would end up on the carpet again. When I asked them to "Please be careful with your drink", it never got spilt.

Since then I have helped hundreds of parents to re-phrase their requests from what they don't want to what they do want, with incredible results.

Some years ago, I worked with a wealthy family whose son seemed to be going off the rails, hanging around with the wrong crowd and generally not doing what he was told. After some initial conversations it became clear that the father of this fifteen-year-old boy was constantly pointing out the pitfalls of mixing with the wrong crowd. He shared with me the conversations he'd had with his son from an early age with regards to the "rough" family who lived down in the village. As he would drive past the "rough" family's house he would point and say to his son, "I'd better not catch you mixing with Jack's son". Can you see how he was drawing attention to the very person he didn't want his son to be spending time with? If we look at the hypnotic language behind the last sentence, he was basically telling his son, "I'd better ~~not~~ catch you mixing with Jack's son". Jack's son had become the pink cat. Guess who he was spending most of his time with as he got older.

Yep! Jack's son.

Another great example of the changes which take place when you choose to ask for what you want was when a mother called me to ask for help with her fifteen-year-old daughter, who in her opinion was hanging around with the wrong crowd, staying out late and generally achieving less than she was capable of at school. Does this sound familiar?

After her daughter had gone out at the end of the second coaching session, I asked the mum, "Out of all the battles you're currently trying to fight, how many are you winning?"

"Now let me see," she said, "There's the untidy room battle, the staying out late battle, the hanging around with the wrong crowd battle and the doing poorly at school battle... Mmm... None!"

She sighed.

"So, if you had to choose ONE battle to win, which would it be?" I asked.

I needed her to become clear on what was most important to her, because as things were at the moment, she just seemed to be moaning at her daughter whatever she did and all her daughter could hear was a constant nagging, moaning drone, and something needed to change.

"I'd want her to stop coming home late," was her reply and as if just to confirm this to herself she repeated, "The battle I'd want to win is for her to stop coming home late."

Now this is an excellent example of a parent focusing on what they don't want. She doesn't want her daughter coming home late.

So, I asked, "What do you say before your daughter leaves the house in the evening?"

She replied with a puzzled look on her face, "I tell her, she's not to come home late, in fact I tell her to be home no later than 10pm."

I also found out that she would often tell her daughter that she was sick of her always being late and treating their home like a hotel. So, if I take those last couple of statements first, this mum is telling her daughter what she doesn't want, and she is also telling her that she treats the home like a hotel. Having navigated two boys through their teenage years, I know that emotions can run high and we sometimes say things that we don't mean, but these kinds of statements only serve to make matters worse. She is effectively hypnotising her daughter to do what she doesn't want her to do! Why would you choose to do that? Well, in fairness, this simple, but effective stuff has not been shared that widely until now. So, you haven't been choosing, you've just been sleepwalking and sleep-talking your way through life. My intention is to give you a gentle nudge, to wake you up and recognise the power you have, quite literally on the tip of your tongue, when you choose your words more carefully.

If you were aware of a different way of communicating, which has been proven to work and would make your life easier and improve your relationships, you'd use it wouldn't you? In fact, by the end of this chapter, it'd be great if you were able to say to yourself, "I'll handle these situations in a more positive and assertive manner."

Back to the story.

What did she in fact want? It took a few attempts, but we finally got to the fact that she wanted her daughter to "come home *before* 10pm".

Why? "Because we love her, and it means her father and I can relax and go to bed at a reasonable hour knowing she's home safely."

I then said, "Next time she goes out with her friends, I want you to tell her what you've just told me."

"But she'll think I'm taking the Mickey," was the reply. "Just do it and see what happens," I insisted.

The following Monday I received a phone call from a very excited mum, who started the conversation with, "It can't be that easy, otherwise everyone would do it!"

"Do what?" I questioned.

"As my daughter was leaving the house on Friday at 6pm to go out with her friends, I said to her, 'Please be home *before* 10pm, because you know your father and I love you very much and it means we can relax and go to bed at a reasonable time.' And you'll never guess what happened – she came home at 9.45pm, fifteen minutes early! That's the first time in the past six months that she's done what she's been told."

But I would put this to you, as I did to that mum on that Monday phone call: You've rarely been telling her what you wanted; only what you didn't want and either way, she gave it to you.

Your life and your relationships will transform when you choose to focus on and ask for what you want, instead of asking for what you don't want. This is a seemingly small but vital change in your language. It may take some practice, especially if you're entrenched in doing it the old way, the fly at the window way, the way that doesn't work.

So just to clarify, I'm suggesting you start to practise the art of focusing and asking for what you want.

I look forward to you sharing your positive stories with me @darrencurtis67 on Instagram or on our Awakened Parent Challenge page on Facebook.

Now, I'd like you to carry
on reading this book!

Chapter

two

Worrying about an if

Worrying about an if...

A lot of teenagers and pre-teens who are referred to me, worry about stuff that might happen in the future or has happened in the past (or at least their version of what has happened in the past). They worry about things like starting school or a new job, commenting, "What if I can't do it?" or "What if I don't know what I'm doing?" They worry about exams, stating, "What if I don't get the results or grades that I need?" and then there's the social side of things, "What if they don't like me?" or "What if I end up on my own at lunchtime?"

This is classic script language. The script will always focus on a '*negative* what-if' and spend a significant amount of time and energy worrying about an event or situation that may not and probably will not happen.

It worries about the smallest detail, as if it were already reality.

The script is so worried about anything that can cause bad feelings that it will imagine every possible worst-case scenario.

Some youngsters' scripts are especially good at doing this, so much so that it worries them sick. Often, you hear people say, "I worried myself sick". No you didn't, your script worried you sick. This tiny shift in language passes the ownership away from you and onto the script. You would not choose to worry yourself sick and nor would your child, but the script would.

One such example was a young girl I was working with called Rachel. Her mum had called me to say that Rachel was nervous to the point of nearly being physically sick and that she was worried she would have to miss her first day at secondary school. When I arrived, Rachel was curled up on the sofa, her knees were tucked up under her chin, her head was down, and it was clear that she'd been crying.

"Fancy a chat?" I said, "Not really" she replied solemnly, because, of course, that's what eleven-year-old girls do!

"Your mum said you were worried about starting your new school tomorrow." I continued, "So what are you thinking?"

She thought for a while, then replied, "What happens if I get split up from my friend?"

Before I could reply, she continued, "What if the teachers don't like me or the lessons are too hard or even worse, I'll probably get lost, because the school is massive."

Once again, I tried to reply, but stopped, sensing Rachel had some more to say (not bad for someone who initially didn't want to talk!)

This time she took a deep breath to enable her Olympic attempt at another sentence. "I probably won't like any of the food at lunchtime and I've heard they bully the new kids if they don't like you and what if I'm forced to sit next to someone I don't like and did I mention that I'm really worried about getting lost?"

I paused for a second before replying, "Those are all valid worries Rachel. However, from the look of you, all these things have already happened."

"I feel sick," she replied.

I handed Rachel a blank sheet of A4 paper and some coloured pens. "Write down exactly how you'd like your first day at school to go, from the moment you get up in the morning. In fact, write it down as if it happened yesterday."

This is what she wrote:

"I woke up yesterday at 6am, excited that it was my first day at secondary school. Mum was calm and Dad had arranged to go to work later so he could be there for me in the morning. My hair looked nice and Mum drove me to school with plenty of time to spare. We picked up Stacey on the way so we could arrive together. We were met by a nice teacher, who gave us a map of the school and showed us where to go. We were shown to our new classroom and my form tutor was really helpful and fun. We played games and I got to know the other kids. I have a great class and made lots of new friends. Lunch was nice and everyone was helpful and friendly. Mum was waiting for me in the car park after school. I called my coach and told him that the whole day had gone much better than I guessed it would."

She smiled when she'd finished writing the letter and said, "But it might not happen like this."

"But what if it does? How great would that be?" I replied.

If Rachel was your child, you can see from what she has written, some of the things that will help her to stay *calm*, like getting up early to give her the time to get ready and look nice. Both Mum and Dad are there to *support* her before school. She also wants the *support* of her friend Stacey on the way to school and finally Mum there to *support* her again at the end of the day. By knowing all of this, it is easier to put these things into place to create a *supportive* environment for Rachel and help calm her nerves. Obviously, this is Rachel's version of a perfect first day. For another youngster, this would be their worst nightmare as they may prefer to walk to and from school with a couple of mates and the further their parents are from things the better. So, each youngster should be treated differently according to what it is *they* want and need.

Back to Rachel's story. I asked her to focus on what she had just written, a '*positive* what-if' instead of the '*negative* what-if' she had previously been discussing. She agreed to focus on the '*positive* what-if' story that made her smile. When she called me the next evening, she said, "The whole day was much better than the script had guessed it would be. It was much more like the story I had chosen to create."

And isn't that often the case, especially during periods of change and uncertainty? The script can sometimes spend so much time and energy worrying about something that *might* happen that it creates a negative picture of the future which is completely false. This is often referred to as False Expectations Appearing Real (FEAR). Whatever the script is most fearful of almost certainly never actually happens. So, what is the point of spending time and energy worrying about it in the first place?

Your time and energy are much better spent creating the future you would choose via a '*positive* what-if' and the best thing of all is that it's actually easier to do, once you get a little practice.

So, when you're next trying to help a child whose script is worrying about a '*negative* what-if', I'd like you to help them turn their focus towards the best possible outcome and focus on their own '*positive* what-if'. The best kind of what-if is "What if things turn out exactly how you'd choose them too?"

Obviously, we don't know what the future may or may not hold for us and so it is fine to plan for certain negative eventualities. However, if that planning is hijacked by the script, it will turn into panic, anxiety, frustration, overwhelm or anger. So, I would strongly recommend you help the individual focus on the best possible outcome, give them the time and space they need to create it, and let them use their own words.

This strategy works for everyone, not just pre-teens and teens. If you're a teacher, try writing out your perfect day at school, from the time you wake up in the morning to the moment you go to bed. How are the kids at school? How are you feeling? What are you thinking about in your perfect day?

If you're a parent, what would a great home-life be like? What time would you get up in the morning? Earlier or later? What time would the kids get up? Would they make their own breakfast, or would you have breakfast as a family? How would your day play out? Would you be there for the kids when they get home from school? Would you like to have dinner together? If so, what time? What would you do differently in the evening?

Just write it all out and be honest and bold. You may even surprise yourself.

> *Our highest endeavour must be to develop individuals who are able out of their initiative to impart purpose and direction in their lives.*
>
> Rudolf Steiner

Playtime

Take a few minutes to imagine and write down what your perfect day was like. Remember to use positive language and past tense, as if it had already happened yesterday.

"My perfect day started yesterday when I...

_____

_____

_____

_____

_____

_____

_____

_____

_____

_____

_____

_____
"

Chapter

three

Motivation

Motivation

A positively framed goal has immense power for our minds to work towards. By positive I mean something along the lines of, "I'd like to have healthy meals together as a family at least four times a week," rather than the negatively framed equivalent: "I want the kids to have fewer take-aways in front of the television". As I've pointed out in the first chapter, *Mind your language*, the latter is focusing on the very thing you don't want, and you are now more aware of how futile that can be – remember the pink cat I asked you not to think about?

Goals are important; they give us and our children something to focus on, something to aim for. They engage the reticular activating system in the brain, which controls what we look for and what we notice. In its simplest form, if you look for problems, you'll find them. If you look for solutions, you'll find them.

So, I urge you to shift your thinking from being a problem-solver to becoming a solution-seeker. They may *sound* like two sides of the same coin, but I can assure you that the difference to your end-result will be significant. I encourage all my students to set what I call a dream goal. I ask them, "If anything were possible, what would you do, be or have?"

I remember working with a group of students in a school near my hometown of Reading in England and one young man called Craig introduced himself to me as the naughtiest kid in the school. A label he wore with some pride. I later found out he wasn't particularly good at sport and he was well below average academically. He would never get recognition in those areas, so winning and gaining attention in the bad behaviour category was something he had found he could excel at!

During the dream goal exercise, I noticed Craig wasn't writing anything down and had started to doodle on his notepad and daydream. I respectfully asked him to share his dream goal with the class. After an initial pause and shrug of the shoulders, as if to say I don't know, he replied, "I wanna be a millionaire". At this point a variety of pens, pencils and rubbers were launched across the room at Craig, accompanied by jeers from his class mates of "You can't even read and write properly, how are you gonna make a million pounds?"

I can imagine those were an accurate reflection of the negative internal voice (the script) that would plague someone like Craig into their adult years and stop them achieving such grand goals, especially if you're not aware that you can separate from the script and consciously choose. (All this is discussed in more detail in Chapter 5.)

Once the room was calmed, I asked Craig when he thought it was realistic to be a millionaire by. He sat up straight and declared that he'd like to be a millionaire by the time he was thirty years old. When you're fourteen, that counts as ancient!

I asked Craig to imagine that it was his thirtieth birthday today and he was walking across his hallway to his front door to collect his mail. "What kind of front door do you have at your home now you're thirty?"

He puffed out his chest with pride and declared, "Well, I built the house myself, so it's a solid oak door with brass fittings".

The class was surprisingly quiet at this point. I think they were in shock because Craig was going along with the scenario instead of playing the fool.

I went on to ask another question. "Amongst all your birthday cards is a letter from your bank containing your bank statement. As you pick it up and open it you are pleasantly surprised by the balance showing in the bottom right hand corner. It says you are one million pounds in credit. Congratulations, you've achieved your goal. You are thirty years old and you have become a millionaire. How does that make you feel?"

Craig took a deep breath, puffed out his chest once more and extended in height by at least six inches, before telling me it felt great. I wanted to help Craig to discover where that feeling might be coming from.

"It's taken you sixteen years and one million pounds, so what has that really given you personally Craig?"

He paused and thought before replying, "It's made my mum really proud..."

I then asked, "That's excellent Craig. Just out of interest, what could you do this week to make your mum really proud?"

Again, he paused before replying, "I suppose I could clean my bloody bedroom up," to which the whole class roared with laughter.

I confirmed with Craig when he would like to clean his bedroom by, and he agreed that the coming weekend would be as good as any.

The following week, his mum stopped me at the school gates to ask what I'd done to her son. When I looked at her in a puzzled way, she continued to tell me that she'd been trying to get him to clean up his room for the past two years, with limited success, until suddenly last weekend he'd cleaned it to the highest of standards without prompting.

"Were you proud of him?" I asked. "Yes, of course," she replied

"Did you let him know you were proud of him?" I continued

"No, I just told him it was about bloody time and he'd better not be expecting any favours in return!"

I shared with her the story I've just told you, about how he came to want to clean his room and, with tears rolling down her face, she mumbled, "I didn't know".

"Please let your son know you're proud of him, because that's all he wants."

Because that's all any youngsters want, especially the "naughtiest kid" in the school. They want their parents and teachers to be proud of them. However, bizarre as it may sound, if they can't find something positive to be great at such as a sport or excelling in a certain subject, they will find something "bad" to be good at, because at least it gets your attention.

Craig was willing to wait sixteen years and amass a million pounds in order to make his mum proud, when there were much simpler, quicker ways to achieve the same goal. Isn't that always the way?

So often, we don't give our children a chance to dream. The script tries to be too practical and realistic, presumably to protect them from being disappointed. In the process we may be squashing our children's dreams before they even get a chance to take root, only for them to lead a life of mediocrity, reaching middle-age and wondering, "Is this it?" Can you see how important it is to let them express what they think they really want? This will enable them to get to what's behind the goal and see what's really driving them.

Never tell people how to do things. Tell them what to do and they will surprise you with their ingenuity.

George S. Patton

Playtime

Which areas of your life is the script causing *you* to put off until tomorrow, that which could easily be achieved today?

_____

_____

_____

_____

If time and money were no object, after you've bought your dream home, all the cars you could ever want and been on multiple vacations, what would *you* be spending your time doing?

_____

_____

_____

_____

How can *you* take one small step towards this today?

_____

_____

_____

_____

Chapter

four

**What's
important to you?**

What's important to you versus what's important to them

Core values

I like to play a little game with the teenagers I work with. The game has only one rule and the rule is: "You can't start until the other person has started." I usually need to repeat this one simple rule a couple of times as my students try to work it out. With a puzzled look on their faces, they exclaim, "But that makes no sense! If I can't start until somebody else has started and they can't start until I have started, then the game will never begin!"

"But surely this is a game you play every day," I reply. The puzzled looks continue, until I explain further.

"I'm not saying sorry until they say sorry or they don't respect me, so why should I show them any respect?" Then I ask them to think of other examples of where in their life this rule keeps showing up.

The result of asking this question to thousands of teenagers has led me to the conclusion that dishonouring the values of respect, freedom, fairness and support seem to be the trigger for many arguments or perceived "bad behaviour".

Each of us has our own set of values. These are what determine which aspects of life we regard as important to us as individuals. Our values help determine what we will spend our time doing, how we spend our money, what hobbies and social activities we pursue.

We each hold many values and our top values are referred to as our core values, as they are at the core of what we stand for. When you give them an order of importance, this will help you to understand your own and your child's decision-making process and motivators.

Often, home and school can become a place of conflict if the values of a teacher do not align with the values of the student. An example would be a teacher who insists, "You're not here to have fun you know." That teacher is going to have a hard time understanding the motivations of a student whose highest value is fun. Similarly, a parent who places a high value on order and organisation will have a hard time understanding a child whose core values are connection and creativity, especially when they drop everything to connect with their friends and their creative style of undertaking homework involves mess and disorder.

In fact, it is our individual values which contribute to us taking action or lead us to inaction, to procrastinate. There are no correct values or better values, because each value will have a unique meaning to each person. Rather than creating conflict by insisting that our values are correct and trying to impose them onto our children, a more sensible thing to do is to live our values daily, enabling our children to understand what is important to us through our actions. However, if you would like to achieve a greater understanding of what makes your child tick and how to get the best out of them, taking the time to discover what your children's values are and learning to work with them to keep them motivated is your key to success.

Generally, teenagers will give respect once they feel it has been given to them and this can cause a significant friction to the third parties involved. However, I've noticed that many adults, especially teachers and parents, seem to play by the same rules, by thinking they are somehow due respect as a pre-requisite of their position or status, and not that it is something to be earned.

From my experience, I have found that by simply showing respect first, it is always reciprocated, even by the most challenging of youngsters. Maybe not immediately but it always follows pretty quickly. Think about this for a second. I'm sure you'll have a value for respect at some level, most people have. In the pursuit of ensuring that value is honoured, you may make the mistake of thinking respect is something that is done to you or that you insist on receiving.

Whereas, I would suggest it is much more useful to view something we value, in this instance "respect", as a triangle, with one side reflecting how much respect you are shown by others, the second side is how much respect you show to others and the third side is how much respect you have for yourself.

> *One has to disrespect oneself to enable others to disrespect them.*
>
> Unknown

Playtime

Please take a minute to complete the following exercise:

On a scale of 0 to 10, with zero being "not at all" and 10 being "all the time", how much self-respect do you have?

On a scale of 0 to 10, how much respect do you show to your children/students?

On a scale of 0 to 10, how much respect do you get from your children/students?

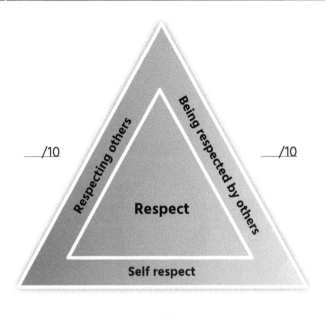

___/10   ___/10

Respecting others

Being respected by others

Respect

Self respect

___/10

If I were a betting man, I would bet that the higher your scores are for your first two answers, the higher degree of respect you are currently enjoying from others.

Somewhere, in a land far away, there was a temple that housed a hall of a thousand mirrors. One day it so happened that a dog got lost in the temple and arrived at this hall. When the dog saw the reflections, he showed his teeth and growled, and a thousand dogs showed their teeth and growled back. The dog was furious that he was not being shown more respect, so he growled even deeper and barked his most fierce bark, and one thousand dogs growled even deeper and barked more fiercely straight back. With this the dog turned and ran with his tail between his legs, thinking that he would never return to such a hostile place ever again.

Sometime later, another dog was similarly lost in the temple. This time, however, when he saw one thousand reflections, he panted and wagged his tail with joy, and a thousand dogs panted and wagged their tails back at him. He barked a playful bark, and a thousand dogs barked a playful bark right back. The dog left with a smile on his face thinking, "What a friendly place, I must come back here often."

You cannot change the level of respect others give you merely by demanding respect, but you can easily increase your self-respect and the respect you show to others. Therefore, if you scored lower than you would have liked on the previous exercise, take some time now to write out what you can start doing today to show more respect to yourself and others. The script may go mad at this point and say, "Why should I show others respect, if they are not willing to show it to me first?" And that's OK, that's what the script does, because it is scared of being taken advantage of. But I believe you would always choose to rise above the script and find a more harmonious solution; maybe one that is better for your blood pressure! And please remember the futility of the game with only one rule, which is the script's favourite game to play. Your only job is to politely tell the script that you no longer wish to play.

I worked with a young man in a school in the south east of England, who was deemed by his teachers to have anger management issues. During one of our early sessions we carried out a values elicitation and found his five core values to be freedom, capability, support, respect, and fun. I asked him to explain the sequence of events leading up to his most recent outburst in class. He told me that he'd been made to feel stupid by his teacher in front of the class. He saw red, swore at the teacher, threw a chair into the wall, and stormed out of the classroom.

> *When our core values are being dishonoured, the script will often cause us to resort to uncontrollable extremes of emotion.*
>
> Darren Curtis (Author)

I asked him what value was being dishonoured to make him react in such an extreme way. "I guess I felt unsupported and disrespected". It's important to remember here that any extreme reaction is a result of our values being perceived to be dishonoured. I say perceived, because the script has its own set of rules telling us when a value is being honoured or dishonoured.

So, a script with a rule that says, "I will only be happy when everyone respects me", is going to be unhappy on a regular basis, because what are the chances of everyone respecting you all of the time? It just ain't gonna happen. So, it's easier if you become aware of these rules and help yourself or the youngster to choose new ones which are easier to achieve. "I always feel respected whenever I show others respect" would be easier to achieve because it's something you are in control of.

I then asked him, "Which of your values was being honoured by acting the way you did?"

His first reply was, "Surely, none of my values were being honoured. I wasn't proud of my behaviour, I wasn't supporting the class or the teacher, it wasn't fun, and I certainly wasn't showing any respect."

"But you were honouring at least one of your values," I continued.

He thought some more, before answering slowly, as if he'd just uncovered a hidden truth.

"I guess I could have been honouring my value of freedom, because I ended up getting out of the class."

I questioned further, "So exactly how much freedom did you get?"

He replied, "I got about two minutes of freedom when I initially stormed out of the class, then I was sent to the deputy head's office, my parents were called and I was sent home, then grounded for the rest of the week."

Now, isn't that interesting, how this young man's script found a highly effective way of getting out of any of his classes where he didn't feel capable or supported. Especially as the ultimate punishment was to be sent home to potentially more freedom (depending on his parents' rules on punishment). And let's face it, even sitting in your bedroom can feel like freedom if you dislike certain teachers or lessons. In the same way, the script will try to keep us safe and make us feel sick on the day when we're due to deliver a big talk or something we don't feel confident with. Think back to Rachel's first day at secondary school, being worried sick. For the record, some of Rachel's core values were safety, support and fun.

This young man's script had found a way to get him "freedom", which would also explain why he said he didn't feel he was in control during the event and he in fact felt guilty afterwards.

I do what I do and asked another question. "What could you choose to do next time you get hijacked by the script and get angry, to ensure you honour your values of respect AND freedom?"

I allowed him the time and space he needed to answer such a question and he eventually replied, "When I get that tight feeling in my stomach, just before I see red, I could just walk out of the class, without disrespecting the teacher or myself". Then almost immediately he added, "Yeah! But that won't work, because I'll still get into trouble for leaving the class."

You'll start to notice that the script always replies with "Yeah! But" whenever you suggest a solution.

"So, what else needs to happen to make it work?" I asked.

Once again there was silence while he thought long and hard, before replying, "I could tell the deputy head the stuff I've just learned and ask her permission to be excused from class for five or ten minutes whenever I see red. That way, all the teachers will know what I'm doing, and I can return to class once I've calmed down and it's better for everyone". Before he'd even finished the sentence, once again his script butted in, "Yeah! But she'll never agree to that."

I replied, "What would you choose?"

That afternoon, he went to the deputy head as agreed, and put the proposition to her. She agreed to a short trial, on the condition that he went to a certain room to cool down where a support teacher helped other children with academic challenges. By a happy coincidence, this honoured his value of support too. He agreed, the trial period was made permanent and I understand that it was rolled out to other pupils with similar issues in school.

Another trigger for your child's negative behaviour (or as we now know, it's the script being triggered, which causes the negative behaviour) can be injustice or perceived injustice. The "problem" child turns up to class five minutes late or does something wrong and the teacher or parent is onto them like a wasp around an open cola can. But when the "A-grade" child walks in five minutes late or does the same thing wrong, everything is fine. We let it go, but why? Because really, we're punishing the "problem" child for all the other stuff stacked up on the script over time. There is a perceived build-up of "disrespect" from them, so hey, if they're not being fair, why should we be fair to them? This comes back to the game with one rule again. Conversely, there's no perceived "disrespect" from the "A-grade" child. Why? Because there isn't loads of negative stuff stored on the script about them.

They haven't dishonoured one of your values; you don't believe they were disrespectful by being late and you're probably right. But the two children have done the same thing, haven't they? So many of my students give many such examples of people or life not being fair. Remember, if their script believes "life isn't fair", they'll create situations which prove them right. Our job is to help prove them wrong and help them to consciously choose beyond what that little negative internal voice is telling them.

I laughed when I was chatting to a good friend of mine over dinner one night, when he recounted a story of how angry he'd got because of the local youngsters having no respect. He went on to tell me that he was walking up a stepped alleyway with a handrail running up the middle. Two youngsters were talking halfway up, and their bikes were blocking his path, forcing him to cross under the handrail and walk on the opposite side of the alleyway. "Bloody teenagers, trying to provoke me, spoiling for an argument," he said, clearly being hijacked by his script

Quite shocked, I replied, "But how do you know that's what they were trying to do?"

"It's obvious, they'd have moved if they'd have been polite. One even said, 'Alright mate?' just to take the piss".

"Surely he realised what he'd done and was trying to make a connection," I explained

His script barked back at me. "No, he wasn't, he was trying to provoke me, so I told him, 'I'm not your bloody mate!'"

So I put it to my friend, "If two elderly gentlemen had met at the same place and were so deep in conversation that they hadn't noticed you until you got right up to them, and as you crossed under the handrail one of them had said 'Alright mate?', would you still have replied, 'I'm not your bloody mate'?"

"Of course not..." he replied.

Our script has different rules for different people who we perceive to be "A-grade" or "A problem".

If you and I can choose to master the balance of respect, freedom, support and fairness, the majority of the youngsters with perceived "problems" will respond positively.

> *Everyone is a genius, but if you judge a fish on its ability to climb a tree, it will live its whole life believing that it is stupid.*
>
> Albert Einstein

Chapter

five

Changing your internal voice – as simple as ABC

Changing your internal voice – as simple as ABC

Many youngsters I talk to are self-conscious and/or lack self-esteem. Not necessarily all the time, but definitely in certain situations, especially when they're unsure. Which let's face it, whether you're six, sixteen or sixty years old, your confidence levels can take a dip whenever you're presented with a situation that you're unsure about. Often a child will have a nagging, doubting, whining voice inside their heads, which makes them negative and either passive or aggressive when it's much better to be positive and assertive.

I hope by now you're starting to realise that this child hasn't got low self-esteem. They are simply reading from the script, and some of the stories on the script tell them all the reasons that they have low self-esteem. The audio version of the script, the negative internal voice, is speaking a little louder than the kind, friendly voice that you would choose to listen to: the voice of confidence, the voice of high self-esteem.

Let me put it another way. If you were listening to a radio station and it was playing music you really didn't like, you'd change the radio station to one which was playing music you love, wouldn't you? So, our job as parents and teachers is to help ourselves and our youth to stop listening to Script FM and tune into Friend FM. There is a significant amount of people who think their radio only plays Script FM because they've never been taught how to change the channel – they have no idea that they have a choice.

The main difference between someone with confidence and someone with low self-esteem is that the person with confidence, just like you and I, still has a negative script to contend with, but they have learned to flip the radio station from Script FM to Friend FM more easily.

The kind, friendly and supporting voice on Friend FM will usually say, "It's OK", "It'll be OK" or "I'm OK."

And that is the secret to being a confident person.

To keep things simple, I get my clients to ask themselves the following question:

"Am I my own best friend or my own biggest critic?"

Just stop and listen to what you're saying to yourself for a second...

I've heard it said, if you talk to yourself, you must be crazy. Well, if that were the case, then the men in white coats are going to be working overtime rounding us all up, because we all talk to ourselves, all the time. Whether you're aware of it or not is a completely different matter. Come on, you certainly don't say everything you think out loud, do you? You'd get in all sorts of trouble, wouldn't you? I know I would!

When you take the time to stop and listen to the thoughts you are thinking, there is a constant chatter going on inside your head. However, most of the time you're so used to your internal dialogue that you don't take any notice of it. At least you don't take any notice consciously but believe me, you're taking plenty of notice subconsciously.

What do I mean by that?

Imagine your internal voice is another person talking to you and, just for a moment, take that voice outside of your head and notice what it would be like to have someone speak to you like you speak to yourself. Is it a friend whispering supportive words, cheering you on and encouraging you or is it a nagging, negative, whining critic who reminds you of past failures, points out your supposed faults, puts you down and generally holds you back? The latter is what I've been referring to as the script. Apologies if it seems I am repeating myself, but I really want you to get how important this is to your relationship with your child and the relationship you have with yourself. Because in my experience, if you have a good relationship with yourself, you'll have an infinitely better relationship with those you love.

I would urge you to listen to how you speak to yourself for a few days and keep a note of what you say. In fact, I dare you to start doing this regularly throughout the day, starting today. Review your comments at the end of each day to check how friendly or critically you are talking to yourself.

Are you listening to Script FM or Friend FM?

This is so important because it helps you to become aware of any negative thoughts, and from that awareness you can change your thinking.

When you change your thinking you change your behaviour, and when you change your behaviour, those around you change theirs.

Once you've become aware, the good news is, you're in charge of what and how you speak to yourself and you can choose to change it at any time. You need to believe me when I say this is the key to a happier, more fulfilling relationship with yourself and your child. It's the bridge between having self-doubt and being self-assured.

One young lady I worked with some years ago, called Jordan, had what is commonly referred to as a negative self-image, low self-esteem and self-loathing. She really didn't like herself and by default, presumed others did not like her either. On the surface she felt like this was something out of her control, something that was almost impossible to change because it was just who she was. Or at least this is what her script told her. And if she were by some miracle able to change, she would have to find out what the problem was and fix it, prior to moving on.

In my experience that could not be further from the truth. I like to keep things simple and use an ABC methodology to help my clients turn down the volume on Script FM and crank up the volume on Friend FM quickly and easily. As mentioned before, the first thing to do is become **Aware**. An example of this could be that you become aware of certain behaviours or aware that other people don't necessarily agree with your way of thinking or aware that there is a solution. Whatever it is, you become aware that you have some form of negative feeling, worry, guilt, sadness, anxiety, frustration, anger etc. You know you are in your script whenever you are experiencing a negative feeling or behaviour.

Then you must **Break** the pattern by doing something differently.

And finally, **Comfort** yourself.

> *If you always do what you've*
> *always done, you'll always*
> *get what you always got.*

Unknown origin

The simplest way I have found to do this with clients like Jordan is to ask them to imagine that we've found a lost little child (imagine a child of three or four years' old) who she must look after for a while. But there are two rules that must be followed if we are to look after this little lost child in a caring and loving way.

The first rule is:
Whenever you are **Aware** of the script saying anything negative to you, you need to say that exact same thing to the child in your care and see how it makes you feel saying that same negative phrase to someone much smaller and much more vulnerable than yourself.

The second rule is:
If you don't like how it sounds saying that negative phrase to the child, **Break** the pattern by re-phrasing it immediately and repeat what you would really like to say to the child to help to **Comfort** them. Once you are happy you have helped the child feel good about themselves, then repeat that same comforting sentence/ phrase back to yourself.

This may sound a bit long-winded, but once you get used to it, you can do it in a matter of seconds.

Jordan agreed to the two rules and we spoke the following week.

She shared that one of the first negative thoughts that she'd been **Aware** of was when she looked in the bathroom mirror the following morning and the script said to her, "You're so ugly, you may as well be dead." She imagined looking into the small child's eyes who I'd asked her to care for and repeated, "You're so ugly, you may as well be dead." After that, she told me she'd burst into tears, as she could hardly believe that she could utter such horrible, spiteful, bullying words to another person, let alone a small child.

She continued to share that she'd wiped the tears from her cheeks, re-phrased the statement to how she'd like to speak to the child. Without a second thought and as if instinctively knowing how to make the little girl feel better, she said, "You are so beautiful, I love you" and with that, she stared back at her own reflection in the mirror, looking straight into her own eyes and repeated to herself, "You are so beautiful, I love you."

Another tear welled up in the corners of her eyes, but these were tears of sheer joy and apparently tasted much sweeter than the bitter tears she was used to, as she confessed to feeling an unfamiliar sense of self-assurance and self-worth coming from inside.

After letting her enjoy the memory of the feeling and the taste of the sweetest tears for a while longer, I asked how it felt saying the first negative statement to the little child and she shared with me that she would never normally speak to a little child like that and it felt completely wrong.

I continued, "So why did you choose to speak to yourself like that?" The answer was quite simple and straightforward: "I wasn't choosing, I was hijacked by the script." She had only just become **Aware**.

Jordan agreed to continue to do this exercise for a while longer, to enable her to become even more Aware of the negative internal script.

During our next conversation, she shared with me what she had caught her script saying when all her friends were meeting up after school one day. It went something like this. "They don't want you tagging along. They only asked you because they feel sorry for you." She immediately stopped herself, imagined she was talking with the little child and repeated that thought/internal dialogue immediately. Once again, she said it sounded and felt terrible saying it to the little child. She confirmed it felt like she was again bullying the child. So, if she feels like she's bullying the little child by repeating what the script was saying, what has the script been doing to her all these years? Jordan immediately re-thought and rephrased what she would like to say to the child. "It'll be OK, just go and enjoy yourself." Wow! What a difference. Jordan went from the script bullying her to being her own best friend and this is the difference between someone you might refer to as having low self-worth or very little confidence, to someone who has self-worth and is more confident. It is quite simply how you would choose to talk to yourself as opposed to how the script talks to you.

When you choose to be your own best friend, talk to yourself positively, encourage and support yourself as a best friend would. You will become more confident and self-assured. After all, you are giving yourself assurance.

> *Self-assurance is simplicity itself: it is the positive, comforting words we choose to use to reassure ourselves internally, which show up as confidence externally.*
>
> Darren Curtis (Author)

Can you see how it is not only your job as a parent or teacher to become **Aware** of your own negative script, **Break** any negative patterns and use **Comforting** words and tones to help you succeed, but also to install this same comforting voice inside your child's head? This is because yours is one of the voices that is already a part of their internal dialogue. We are all script readers and script writers. So, the second important thing you need to ask yourself, when thinking about the way you speak to your child, is, "Am I talking to them like their best friend or their biggest critic?"

How do I currently talk to myself? Am I listening to Script FM or Friend FM?

Playtime

Complete the following sentence:

Life is...

I am ...

If you answered positively, that's great. If your script answered negatively, what would you choose to replace those beliefs with?

Life is...

I am ...

When you change your thinking you change your behaviour, and when you change your behaviour, those around you change theirs.

Darren Curtis (Author)

Chapter

six

Is it true or not?

Is it true or not?

Have you heard of the placebo effect?

A placebo is a sugar-coated pill containing no drug, which is given to a control section of patients to test the validity of a drug being tested. This enables the laboratory to compare the results between:

a) people who were given the drug
b) people given the placebo
c) people given nothing at all

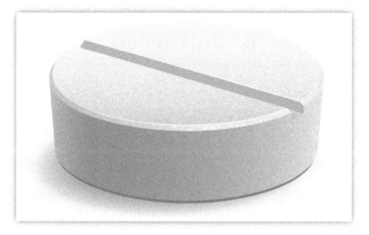

It is scientifically accepted that a significant proportion of the patients taking the placebo will experience an improvement in their symptoms. The only explanation for this is the power of their mind, as they *believe* they have been given the drug which will help their symptoms; therefore, their symptoms improve.

It is also scientifically accepted throughout sports psychology that it is just as important (if not more so) to train the mind to be successful and achieve results. The most successful athletes and sports professionals spend time imagining their desired outcome in their mind as well as training their bodies to be physically prepared. If they didn't believe they could win, it is unlikely they would, no matter how physically fit they were.

My first experience of this was when I was struggling to achieve anything better than third place in the 800-metre running event at school. My form tutor at the time was Mr Pritchard and he advised me to imagine, prior to training each morning, how I would run the perfect race and see myself crossing the line in first place. I then became attached to what the experience of winning would feel like.

When it came to the race, on the basis of experience and on paper, there were two other guys who had better times than me, so they were certainly the favourites to win on the day. However, every morning for the previous month, I had imagined running a better race than these two guys. This meant that in my mind I'd already done it, I'd already imagined winning. I'd already imagined the excitement of being the first to cross the finishing line. On the day of the race I stood on the starting line in the position I'd imagined and ran the race exactly as I'd visualised, staying only inches behind my two main competitors as we went around the track, until we came to the final bend, when I overtook them and sprinted for all I was worth on the final straight to win the race, not by a small amount, but by the significant margin I had visualised.

I trust you'll agree that your mind is a powerful tool. However, be clear that you can make it work for you or against you (if the script is allowed to whisper in your ear unchecked). Harnessing the knowledge that it can make a positive difference, use it to help your children to create a powerful and positive subconscious mind for themselves. A friendly internal voice that more easily says, "I'm OK", "It's OK" or "It'll be OK".

Our minds work on two levels, consciously and subconsciously.

PSYCHOLOGY WARNING! Do not read the next few paragraphs unless you want to understand your child and yourself a little better!

Your conscious mind is the part of your mind responsible for logic and reasoning. If I asked you about the sum of two plus two, it's your conscious mind which is going to be used to add the two numbers together.

Your conscious mind also controls the actions you take with intention while being conscious. For example, when you decide to make any voluntary action like moving your arm or leg to make yourself more comfortable, you have consciously decided that you feel uncomfortable and by moving your arm or leg into a different position you will feel more comfortable, so this is being initiated by the conscious mind.

Whenever you are aware of the action you are undertaking, you can be confident that you are doing it with your conscious mind. If there is a drink beside you and you decided to take a sip, this process will be being taken by your conscious mind because you were 100% conscious while doing it.

The conscious part of your brain is also known to be the gatekeeper for your mind. If someone tried to present you with a belief, criticise you or call you a name, you consciously filter according to your current belief system whether it is true or false before letting it in.

If, for example, someone told you that you are "stupid", your conscious mind will filter this statement depending on your current belief system. If you believe you are stupid, the statement is allowed past the gatekeeper to support your existing belief: "Yes I am stupid, here's even more evidence, another person is confirming I'm stupid." Alternatively, if you currently believe you are clever, your gatekeeper will question the statement/criticism as being false and either completely disregard the information or push the onus of the mistaken statement/criticism back onto the person making the statement: "They are wrong." This then supports your current belief, "I am clever".

This is why you will often hear me referring to the fact that we are all trying to prove ourselves right all of the time. We are trying to prove ourselves right based on a set of beliefs about ourselves, others, and the world around us, which may or may not be true.

What is the subconscious mind?

Your subconscious mind is the part of your mind responsible for your involuntary actions. Your heartbeats and breathing rate are controlled by your subconscious mind. If you become aware of your breathing, your conscious mind will take charge and you will start to consciously breath. Just as with the suggestion of a pink cat, I bet, as you are reading this that you have suddenly become conscious of your breathing and probably just took a deep breath. Once you relax and forget about your breathing, your subconscious mind takes charge and you start to breath subconsciously again.

Your emotions are also controlled by your subconscious mind. This is why you may sometimes feel afraid, anxious, frustrated, angry or down without wanting to experience such a feeling. Whenever you feel a negative feeling, this is also a warning that you have been hijacked by the script! You may have a money script, a health script, a relationship script, a religious script. You'll know which script you've inherited from your parents, grandparents, teachers, care givers etc. Because you'll start to notice what creates a negative feeling for you. Often, it's our children that hold up a mirror and reflect what's on our script. And remember, they have a script too and an argument can only happen when two people's scripts clash. If someone is in the script and you can choose to remain calm, then an argument cannot happen, because you are consciously choosing your emotions.

> *Just because you're invited to an argument, you don't need to accept!*
> Richard Wilkins

Your subconscious mind is also the place where your memories and beliefs are stored. Most of the challenges you or your child will be experiencing are because of one or more limiting beliefs stored subconsciously on the script. We all have limiting beliefs written on our script; it's just that some are more limiting than others.

The good news is, you can consciously choose to put the script down from time to time, take a deep breath and be your own best friend; remember the story about Jordan in Chapter 5.

I have been studying psychology, Neuro Linguistic Programming (NLP) and hypnosis for many years and I came to the conclusion a long time ago that most of the psychological challenges people face can be traced back to limiting beliefs they've been handed in the script!

Self-confidence can be improved by choosing your beliefs about your abilities, skills, and identity.

Trust issues can be resolved by choosing above and beyond what the script would have you believe about perceived injustice and/or being mistreated in your past.

Self-image can be enhanced by focusing on and accepting that you are loved more than you could ever know for who you are right now, without the need for being thinner, fatter, taller, shorter, cleverer, more organised, less organised or whatever else the script tells you that you need to be to be a better person. These were all written on your script a long time ago. It's not who you are, and it's OK to let go; you are who you'd choose to be. The real you is simply you, minus the script. You don't need to be anything more, you just need to turn the volume down on Script FM, put your hand on your heart and ask, "What would I choose to believe right now?"

Another useful way to override a limiting belief on the script is to convince the conscious mind logically to accept that it is limiting, in effect questioning its validity. Then create a more empowering belief to replace it. The trick is to start noticing and gathering evidence to support the new empowering belief, enabling it to pass the gatekeeper into the subconscious mind.

To achieve personal growth for you and your child, the best thing you can do is to understand the combined power of the conscious and the subconscious mind working together.

One of the best demonstrations of this is to show how emotions can be more easily chosen.

The trigger for your negative emotions is subconscious, it's on your script and the script would have you believe it can be difficult to stop them. However, knowing that your bad thoughts (how the script talks to you negatively) are processed through your conscious mind and that your bad thoughts are the primary trigger for your emotions, you can easily choose how you speak to yourself and in turn control your emotions. Remember, if the script is in charge, as it will be from time to time, you are not talking to yourself, you are being spoken to by the script.

> *The only difference between "I can" and "I cannot" is a "not" and you want to avoid "nots", because "nots" only help you hold onto things, they don't help you to let go and move forward.*
>
> Darren Curtis (Author)

I love working with teenagers because they seem to be more accepting of new ideas. They absorb information without necessarily seeking to make complete sense of it. This means that they often just take action and therefore then obtain fast results. Here is a story which may help to clarify and instil the information from this chapter into your subconscious mind more easily.

I was asked to work with a young teenage boy called Carlos. His step-mum was concerned he was extremely quiet and spent most of his time out with friends or in his room, and therefore very little time with the family. She had presumed from this that he may be resentful towards her because he'd been forced to move from his own home abroad, where his real mother lived with his younger brother, or maybe he was jealous of the relationship she had with his father or was it that he just didn't like her as a person? Can you see how all of these are scenarios created by the script?

Because, we don't know if any of these beliefs or assumptions are true, but as this was her script's current perception of the situation, you can see how it might affect how she reacted with worry, frustration, anger or sadness. All of which are unhelpful states of mind to be in.

I'm not a therapist or counsellor, so it wasn't my job to get to the core of these issues. In any case, in my experience teenagers don't want things to get all heavy and serious. It's my job to help teenagers and parents to find the most simple and effective solutions and ways forward. The only way to find out what was really going on in Carlos's head was to have a chat.

During the first session, Carlos shared with me that he found it impossible to talk to his step-mum. So, Carlos's *limiting* belief on the script he was given was, "I find it impossible to talk to my step-mum". When our script holds a *limiting* belief about something or someone, we search for evidence to prove ourselves right. So in Carlos's case he would go straight to his room after school, go out with friends for as long as possible, and basically spend as little time as possible with his step-mum, therefore cementing his script's belief that he found it impossible to speak to her.

I asked whether he liked the fact that he found it impossible to speak to his step-mum. His reply was quick and to the point, "No, of course not, but it's the truth". And this is a valuable lesson to us all. Our script always seems to be the truth to us, because as I pointed out earlier, we spend our lives searching for evidence to prove to ourselves that what is written on our script about our identity, life and other people is in fact true. Often, it couldn't be further from the truth!

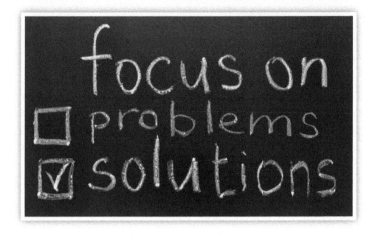

I went on to ask Carlos, "If I was to return in a couple of weeks and you could talk to your step-mum, what might your new belief be?"

His reply after a little encouragement was, "I suppose I would say something like, I find it easy to talk to my step-mum."

I continued, "Ok, if you did find it easy to talk to your step-mum, what sort of things would you do differently?"

I'm asking this question, because I want to bypass the script's childlike "but it's not true" type of response, to enable him to even consider the question before allowing him to give himself the answer.

Carlos initially looked down, before snapping his head up and answering, "Well, I know Dad wants us to spend more time together as a family, so I guess I'd suggest we could all go to the cinema. That way, Dad would be pleased because *I'd* made the suggestion, I'd feel more comfortable, because you don't need to talk while you're in the cinema and then we could chat about the film on the way home."

I don't know about you, but I thought that was a great solution and compromise.

I asked again, "What else would you do as you begin to find it easier to talk to your step-mum?"

Carlos replied, "Well, she's quite clever, so I guess I could ask her to help me with certain course work I'm struggling with."

I persisted in helping Carlos to find options by asking, "What else?" over and over.

Carlos continued to build a picture of what life would be like *if* he found it easy to speak to his step-mum.

This helped to show him a) it was possible and b) it was potentially a good thing and something he could see a benefit in doing. It was all about making the whole thing more acceptable to the gatekeeper in his mind.

Obviously, at this early stage, Carlos was still listening to that old belief and his old belief was still the truth to him, as he had no real evidence to the contrary.

To ensure the *new* belief had the best chance of taking root and growing, we needed to anchor it into his unconscious, through his conscious mind. Like any new skill/behaviour, the more you practise, the better you get.

It is the same when it comes to changing a belief. So, I asked Carlos what he did at least twelve times every day. He confirmed that he checked his mobile phone or sent text messages regularly throughout the day, so this would become his anchor, the thing that would remind him to repeat to himself his new belief, "I find it easy to talk to my step-mum". He confirmed that he was totally committed to saying his new belief throughout the coming days and weeks, especially whenever he checked his phone or received a text.

Why do we need to use this anchoring technique? Whilst the script still believes the old belief is true, it will conveniently help us to forget to do the things we've promised to do. I'm sure you can think of a time when you've been trying to lose weight or exercise more, only to find yourself forgetting to buy the salad from the shop or double-booking the time you'd set aside for your exercise class. This is because you were hijacked by your script, basically proving your old beliefs right and returning to your old pattern of behaviour. Unfortunately, the script doesn't like change; it thinks it is keeping us safe by not changing and sticking to what is familiar.

So, anchoring just jogs our memory. It reminds us we have committed to a new way of doing things, that we have a new empowering belief to install. I am not suggesting that the affirmation of "I find it easy to talk to my step-mum" is magically creating the change. However, from my experience, it keeps the awareness of the desired change in the forefront of your conscious mind and helps you to find the solutions you need to start supporting the new belief. This ensures you start to let the new evidence past the gatekeeper and thus give the new empowering belief a quicker route to your subconscious mind.

Two weeks later, I rang the doorbell and Carlos's step-mum answered the door. "What have you done to Carlos?" she said, smiling from ear to ear.

I laughed and asked what she meant. "Well, he's changed, he's much more talkative and sociable".

"Let me chat to Carlos and see what he's got to say about it," I replied.

I went through to the lounge, where Carlos was sitting. We shook hands and Carlos smiled one of those knowing smiles.

"So, what's been going on?" I asked.

He replied, still smiling, "We went to the cinema, which was great. We've been out for a family meal and I've also spent more time sitting and chatting with the family at dinner time. My step-mum has helped me with a few bits of course work and we've been getting along really well, it's been a really great couple of weeks."

"So, what's changed?" I enquired.

"I guess I've just found it easier to talk to my step-mum", he replied.

He went on to say that not only had he been saying his new belief when he checked his phone, but he'd been saying it to himself when he cleaned his teeth in the morning and whenever he'd thought of it during the day, because it always made him laugh.

Carlos had successfully broken the pattern of the limiting belief written on his script and replaced it with a more empowering belief, which meant he was starting to find evidence to support the new belief. This effectively allowed him to come up with new ways of doing things which would not have been possible had he continued to allow his script to focus on his old belief.

Change the way you look at things and the things you look at change.

Dr Wayne Dyer

To me, beliefs are like pathways through the forest of your subconscious mind. Some of those pathways are well trodden and those particular pathways seem to be the only way to get to where you're going. However, once you become aware that some of your script's pathways are causing you problems and limiting where they can take you, I presume you'd be open to the suggestion of creating a new pathway through the forest? This may be a bit of challenge at first, because you're not used to walking this new path. However, the more often you use it, the more well-trodden it becomes until, before you know it, your script's old pathway is overgrown and your new pathway is the easiest way to get to where you want to go. In fact, it'll be difficult for you to remember where the old pathway was, let alone why you ever used it in the first place. This is one more example of how to turn the volume down on Script FM.

> *You may think the grass is greener*
> *on the other side, but if you*
> *take the time to water your own*
> *grass it will be just as green.*

Darren Curtis (Author)

Playtime

When you get hijacked by your script, what type of things might it say to you?

1._____

_____

_____

_____

2._____

_____

_____

_____

3._____

_____

_____

_____

When you're in a calm and loving mood, what would you choose to believe about yourself?

1._____

_____

_____

_____

2._____

_____

_____

_____

3._____

_____

_____

_____

Chapter

seven

Pain and pleasure are the catalyst for change

Pain and pleasure are the catalyst for change

You can't force your child to change; you can only help them to change if they're ready and willing. As the saying goes, "You can lead a horse to water, but you can't make it drink." Basically, they need to have a good enough reason to *want* to change.

If I were a sports coach and my client wanted to lose weight and get a toned physique to run faster or jump higher, we would probably work on a certain diet and exercise programme which would get them fitter and toned. If they didn't then do the exercises we agreed upon and carried on eating an unhealthy diet, nothing would change. As my good friend and mentor Tony Robbins taught me long ago, people will only change their behaviour when either the end result (their goal) is pleasurable enough or the pain of their current situation is bad enough to make them consistently and permanently take the necessary actions to change their current pattern of behaviour.

As human beings, we are basically driven to take action by moving towards pleasure or away from pain or a combination of the two. Think of it like this: Why do you go to work? Is it because you love it, therefore it's for the pleasure, or is it because you have bills to pay and the thought of not being able to fulfil your commitments is not acceptable to you?

Bearing in mind that the ultimate outcome of not paying your bills is to become homeless, I presume this really doesn't appeal to you. In which case you are moving away from the pain (shame or embarrassment) it would cause you to not honour your commitments (or to be homeless).

You may well work to pay the bills, but actually you enjoy the social side of going to work and therefore one part of you is moving away from pain, while the other part of you is moving towards pleasure.

It is for this reason that I get fulfilment from working with youngsters who are being bullied. That sounds terrible I know, but it's true, because my job is made so much easier because their pain is so bad that they are willing to try anything to stop the bullying.

There are several ifs and buts when trying to help a youngster who is being bullied. Firstly, they need to trust you enough to confide in you that there is a problem. By trust, I not only mean trust that you will listen, trust that you will give the situation the significance it deserves, but trust that you won't take the situation into your own hands and try to deal with things on their behalf, potentially making a bad situation a whole lot worse for them.

So, when you find yourself...

in the privileged position of a young person sharing with you that they are being bullied, listen, and listen some more. Listen to the words they use, because they are the words you'll need to use back to them to show them you understand. An important distinction here is that you must understand their exact words, not your interpretation of what they have said.

Find a quiet spot where they'll feel safe enough to continue and commit to being 100% present with them through this. If you haven't got the time to do this now, then you need to put aside a time later that same day to go through it. Personally, I would drop everything to let a child talk to me about bullying, as it will have taken a lot for them to open up enough to ask for help. I'm always careful to take these opportunities as soon as they are presented to me rather than putting them off.

Our job, if we really want to help them get through this, is to encourage them to come up with their *own* solutions rather than our suggested solutions. If you set out your opinion or your solution to the problem, you are just another adult who doesn't really understand. Although the young person will say, "I know, I know", they are in fact highly unlikely to take your advice, let alone act on it.

In my experience, when somebody says, "I know", that really means, "I've just stopped listening".

Once they have shared with me that they're being bullied, I say something like, "So how many people are at your school?" They obviously reply with a figure, let's say a thousand for the sake of this example.

I go on to ask, "So does this person bully all one thousand students at your school?"

"No" is always the reply.

I continue with a friendly smile on my face. "So, what's so great about you, that they've chosen to bully you?" Now this last sentence may seem harsh, but it's designed to break the pattern of negative emotion and get them to start questioning things a little.

Can you see how that is better than using victim language like, "Oh! You poor thing", which is not helpful and only serves to make them feel sorry for themselves and seek solace in the script.

Now, the bully could be bullying them for all sorts of reasons. It could be that they've got a certain hair or skin colour, a big nose, they're too fat, too thin, too tall, too short, too rich, too poor, too clever, too stupid, the list is endless.

In my experience this just gets them ready for the next exercise, which is the part, if done correctly, that will work every time and helps them to help themselves. It does this by changing their perception of the situation and their perception of the bully and their role in that particular relationship, because bullies only bully people whose script allows them to be bullied.

The best way I have found to help them come up with their own solution is an NLP (Neuro Linguistic Programming) technique called 'perceptual positioning' or the 'meta mirror'. This is a simple but incredibly powerful technique to help to change a person's perception or view of a situation or relationship. It involves disassociating from the experience so they can see things from a different perspective.

The steps

Position 1: Seeing the situation through their own eyes
Position 2: Seeing the situation through the eyes of the bully
Position 3: Looking at the situation as a third party
Position 4: Seeing the situation through their own eyes, with new learning

The process

Position 1: Help them to imagine standing in front of the person they are being bullied by as if they were really there. Ask them to be themselves and tell the bully exactly how they feel. Ask them what they're thinking, confirm what they think the problem is. If they cry, let them cry, it's all good, but if they are crying do not touch them or try to console them, as you don't want to anchor that negative feeling. Just let them have their moment.

When they have said absolutely everything they want to say, get them to shake their arms and legs. This may sound strange, but it enables them to shake off that particular state. Now direct them to stand in position 2.

Position 2: Stand them in the place where they imagined the other person to be. This is usually directly opposite position 1. Now encourage them to stand the way the bully stands and act like the bully acts, use the voice of the bully and pretend to be the bully. This pretend version of the bully has just heard everything they said to them in position 1, so now it's the bully's chance to respond. Just encourage them to say whatever comes to mind, everything they think the bully would say.

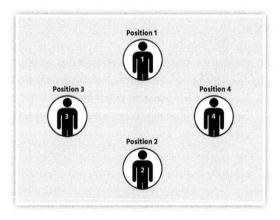

When they have said everything they want to say as the bully, encourage them to shake their arms and legs again to break their state and to shake off "being the bully". Then direct them from where they were standing and into position 3. This should be adjacent to position 1 and 2, creating the points of a triangle.

Position 3: Now stand them in a position where they can 'see' the interaction that went on between themselves and the bully. Encourage them to say what they are thinking and feeling as they look at the scene, having heard what was said by both parties.

When they have answered the questions about what they are thinking and feeling, ask them to shake their arms and legs again to break that state once again. Direct them into position 4. This is next to position 1, as if they were whispering into their own ear, when they were in position 1.

Position 4: In this position they can gain a view on all three positions as though they were not involved at all. They can pretend to be a fly on the wall or an expert in the field of bullying. Ask them what they would recommend or what advice would they give to themselves in position 1. When they have finished talking, encourage them to shake their arms and legs to break the state once again.

Get them to go back to where they started in position 1 and ask them how they feel now. How do they view the situation, ask them what's changed, what does the bully look like now.

The result

From experience, the youngsters I go through this exercise with will come up with the best advice for themselves. It may be the same advice that you would have suggested, but by allowing them to come up with their own solution, they will follow through with it. Their script may still be fearful or apprehensive, but if done correctly, they will now have a different perception of the bully. The bully will be less significant, smaller, they may even feel sorry for them. They will have changed their role in the relationship with the bully from that of a victim to that of someone in a more powerful position. The bully will find it difficult to bully this individual anymore because, as I mentioned before, the bully will only pick on those individuals whose script allows them to be bullied. You will have helped the youngster change on the inside. When you change on the inside, the results show on the outside.

This is a simple, powerful, and effective technique to assist that internal perceptual change. Like any new skill, it will take some practice to get it right. Get together with a group of other parents or teachers and practise with one another.

Alternatively, you can log onto **www.darrencurtis.com/challenge** to find out when our next workshops are, where we can show you an example of how it works.

The sad thing is...

I think it's worth remembering that any type of bullying is a cry for help. If the bully's script is finding so many faults in others and is managing to make other's lives that miserable, just stop and think what their script must be saying to them. Imagine what is going on or has gone on in the bully's life that their script is so afraid of letting go and asking someone for help. And believe me when I say they desperately need help, because they are the dog that barks and growls in the hall of a thousand mirrors.

They've become so used to people's scripts growling and barking back, they think it's normal. The trick here is to break the pattern and wag your tail. Do the opposite of what they expect, look for the good and when you find it (which you will), let them know you have noticed it. Remember, they're just looking for someone to be proud of them too. They've just forgotten how easy it is to achieve.

I'm conscious that social media is a huge part of most teenagers' lives, so I've invited my good friend Heather Miller, founder of the kindness hub (**www.thekindnesshub.com**), to write the following section.

There are thousands of books on cyberbullying that go into a great deal of depth. What I want to do here is to give you some insights of what the online world looks like from the perspective of a teenager.

Having this perspective and understanding will help you to conduct open and informed conversations with your young people which builds trust instead of destroying it.

When you were growing up, do you remember making friends out in the playground? You had a set of unwritten rules for how to act, who to talk to first, what to do. Well, the same is true in cyber life. There are endless, changing, unspoken 'rules' on how someone is meant to show up online. These include but are not limited to 'what being a good friend/boyfriend/girlfriend' looks like. It is a difficult world to fully understand, but what could seem completely unimportant from the outside, such as confiscating a phone, could be an emotional travesty for a teenager.

So often, we as parents think the answer to behavioural management is to just confiscate the phone. To take it forcefully overnight. It makes sense, especially if it seems the problems are coming from there. Sadly, this action does not build trust between you and your teenager; instead, it erodes it.

Think of a phone as being similar to a teenager to a lifeline. I know this sounds absurd, but it is their vital connection to their friends, community, world and a lot of the time, their identity. I'm not saying this is a good thing. But what I am saying is that forcefully taking it away won't create the change in behaviour you are hoping for. Instead, it will erode the relationship between the two of you. As an alternative approach, I recommend creating boundaries together and that is where these insights really come in handy.

Create simple rules such as no phones in the bedroom after a certain hour or no phones at the dinner table. Monitoring what accounts they follow on various platforms and checking in really makes a world of difference. Coming to these decisions together though, with compromise on both sides, is essential. It shows them that you value their opinion.

Let's take Snapchat as an example:

On Snapchat you have the ability to create 'streaks' with people you interact with. A streak is maintained when you and your friend both send each other a picture or video on consecutive days. I have spoken to young people who have more than 365 days of streaks with their friends. That's a year of habitual and mutual effort on both accounts.

This may sound silly and time-consuming, but to someone who this is important to, if you were to take their phone away for a day, they would lose this 'streak' and then be incredibly upset and embarrassed. They'll feel like you don't care or understand and their friend on the other end will most probably give them a hard time about it as well.

Translation: You become the bad guy.

Whereas, if you were to sit down and have a conversation about what could be acceptable usage times etc., this would be a far more constructive approach.

Here is a quick tour through some of the other platforms.

Facebook: Teenagers today don't really use FB anymore as it's more of a Generation Y and upwards platform.

Messenger: You don't need FB to have Messenger. Teenagers usually have it but are more likely to be texting or using DMs (Direct Messenger) on Instagram.

Instagram: Instagram is the most likely platform your teenager is using. They in fact most probably have two accounts. One for the public and family and one called a 'burn account' that is just for close friends where they post some 'behind the scenes' style of photos and videos. This account will most certainly be set on private. And you can't blame them really; you would not have wanted your family eavesdropping into everything you were doing with your friends when you were their age, would you?

TikTok: This is a relatively new platform really spreading its wings in the 2020s. It's all about sharing videos that trend in different topics. There is everything on there from Kindness Challenges to dancing and, inevitably, things young people really shouldn't be looking at! Most youngsters I know use it quite creatively.

YouTube: For a teenager who has grown up with this all their lives, being connected online is very important to them. They haven't experienced a world where they do not have this type of access to information and 'friends' at their fingertips. It's their community. When a teenager is following their favourite YouTuber online, it's not just a video. It's something they feel to be a part of, it's an identity, a movement. The comments are an opportunity to connect, feel seen, and heard.

However, sometimes these commenting forums can lead to online bullying and the worst humanity has to offer. It is a place where people do not associate comments as actually coming from other 'people'. It is therefore so important to teach our teenagers how to disengage. This is so that, when things get heated, they know that they have the option to leave. We have an amazing opportunity to support them in knowing what is real and what isn't. What is worthy of engagement with and what is not. You also have the opportunity to block certain people, otherwise they'll just end up arguing with their script.

The important thing to understand about the online world in all of this is that it's not about the platform, it's about how well we equip the person. The same techniques in this book that apply to building the self-confidence and trust of your teenager apply to the online world. I just really wanted to include this in here, so you feel knowledgeable and mindful when making rules around technology and are aware of some of the 'hows' to assist you in doing that.

There absolutely needs to be guidelines in place for the way our teenagers use their online time. The way in which you go about creating these guidelines with them will be a contributor to their life-long learning and add to the strength of your relationship. This means that when something does come up online that they are not comfortable with, they know they can come to you and have a conversation with a caring parent, not their script.

I wish my parents had told me you don't need to accept everyone you know as "friends" on social media. If they're not your true friend, and you wouldn't sit down and talk about their life, you're both just using each other to look popular, and be nosy. Enjoy a simple and empty feed, it's better for your mental health.

A teenager who was bullied online.

When kids start to share something about what they are experiencing, don't be quick to start blaming yourself if you hear something that may be 'hurting' them, as you'll stop hearing them. Sit with them, let them share, get curious. Don't make it about you!! Another thing would be, don't make the mistake of thinking it wouldn't be your kid.

A parent of a child who was bullied online.

Playtime

What is causing you the most pain at the moment?

_____

_____

_____

What would you like to let go of right now?

_____

_____

_____

What gives you the most pleasure at the moment?

_____

_____

_____

What baby steps could you take towards this today?

_____

_____

_____

Chapter

eight

Praise their identity, discipline their behaviour

Praise their identity, discipline their behaviour

What you tell a child they are, is what they become. Tell a child they're stupid, irresponsible and a waste of space, and that will be written on the pages of that child's script and they will live down to your expectation.

Tell them they are amazing, they can be whatever they want to be, they're loved no matter what, and that will be absorbed into every fibre of their being and they will live up to your expectation.

The voices of people who are significant to them, parents, teachers, guardians, siblings, close friends, or carers, become the voices in their heads when they have a decision to make.

When someone offers them a drug or cigarette or to get into a stolen car, unconsciously they'll refer to their internal dialogue and ask, "What would a stupid person do?", "What would a waste of space do?", "What would an irresponsible person do?", and perhaps take the drug or cigarette or steal the car.

"What would an amazing person do?", "What would a person who is loved and secure do?" By asking these types of questions, more than likely they will say, "No thanks, I'm OK".

When my son smashed the double-glazed window at the back of our house, he came to me in tears and said, "Dad, I'm really sorry, I broke the window". Now I could have said, "*You* stupid idiot, how many times have I told you *not* to play football near the windows at the back of the house?" Does that sound like something you're likely to say when you're angry or annoyed? I know I may have done so before I knew about all this stuff.

Well, it's worth noting my points from Chapter One, the pitfall of telling them what you don't want. Take away the word "not" in the previous statement and I would have been planting the seeds for my son "to play football near the windows at the back of the house". Also, I would have been attacking his identity by saying "*you* stupid idiot". Is that really a belief about his identity I want to put on his script and for him to carry around for the rest of his life? And I would have effectively been punishing him for coming to me and telling the truth. What good would that do? Make him feel even worse, make him feel it's not good or safe to tell the truth?

In fact, what I said was, "That was very honest of *you* – I really appreciate it when you're honest with me. I really appreciate that you are such an honest person. Can you see now why I tell you to play football at the end of the garden?" Are you reading this, and your script has started to say, what a pushover? I can assure you, I'm no pushover and I'm all for the punishment fitting the crime, but let's be realistic here, what would my script have been getting angry about? The cost of the replacement window, the time and hassle of replacing the window, or the fact that he hadn't listened to me about playing at the rear of the garden (which some may perceive as being disrespectful or irresponsible). I went on to say, "So how are we going to pay for this?"

Bailey replied, "Well I guess I need to pay for it out of my pocket money."

I have a high value of fairness and it would have upset me to think of him paying the full price of replacing the window. I know that I wouldn't have followed through on such a punishment, and this would have sent him the wrong message, but I did want to teach him a life lesson. So, I thanked him for his offer and said I felt it was fair if we paid half each, considering how honest he'd been.

We all make mistakes and sometimes we are punishing our children because they reflect back to us our own mistakes logged on our script and how those mistakes made us feel. We find our script is overreacting because they have dishonoured one or more of our core values (e.g. respect, care, control, safety etc) or we simply have too much to do and they have just added to our stresses. However, that's not *their* problem is it?

In this instance, Bailey was still punished for his mistake, but the cost was now only £47.50, and it did not damage his confidence, self-esteem or create a fear of being able to admit he'd made a mistake. Can you see how a few small changes in your reaction will make a huge difference to your child's long-term emotional well-being? Your script will always react negatively, but with some practice you will start to consciously choose how to respond calmly, assertively and kindly.

> ### *A catch-all statement is, "I love you, but your behaviour is unacceptable."*

When my kids used to leave for school in the morning I say, "Enjoy yourselves, have a great day, learn lots, I love you."

When I was working at the University of California San Diego, I would go down the steep hill to the beach early in the morning to walk, relax and watch the surf dudes catching the early morning waves. On my way back to campus one morning, going back up the steep hill, I overtook a grandmother with her granddaughter trailing behind. I couldn't help overhearing their conversation:

"Nanny I'm tired, my legs are aching."

"You're lazy," the grandmother's script replied, as she picked up her granddaughter.

I politely interrupted, hoping to help. "No, she's not lazy, she's got lots of energy."

I raised the issue with the grandmother of the importance of identity. I raised with her that there was a deadening power to the "You're lazy" label. I suggested that there could be a different outcome if she were to give her granddaughter a label of something more positive like "You're strong" or "You're a little bundle of energy".

The granddaughter's ears had been flapping all the time we'd been talking. She suddenly jumped out of her grandmother's arms and sprinted the last 30 metres to prove to us how much energy she had, shouting, "I'm strong and I'm a little bundle of energy". Her grandmother was grateful for my friendly observations and asked me why this sort of stuff isn't taught in schools. I don't have an answer to that question, but I'm sure it will be one day, when the decision-makers catch up.

Children are sponges waiting to absorb life's experiences and learnings, which is why we have to be careful what we say to them and how we say it, as it is our words, and the words of the script which we unconsciously pass down to them, that shape their identity.

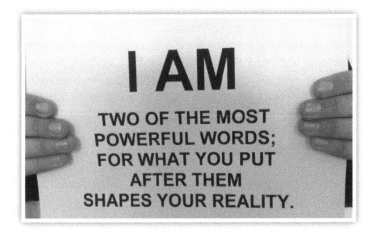

I AM

TWO OF THE MOST
POWERFUL WORDS;
FOR WHAT YOU PUT
AFTER THEM
SHAPES YOUR REALITY.

Remember, if your script tells a child that he/she is stupid, then they will think they are stupid. "Stop trying and act stupid." Yours is the voice they'll hear inside their heads in their moments of decision in the months and years to come. Just like you and I, our children make thousands of decisions which become ever more challenging: "Should I say yes to this drug I'm being offered?" or "No, I'm fine thanks". If your child isn't behaving how you would like them to, then think back to some of the phrases you've used, or your script has used, to describe them – are they positive or negative? Good or bad? If you said it from the heart, chances are it's positive and good. If you were hijacked by your script, chances are it will have been bad and negative.

Here is a story to help to illustrate this.

I was chatting with a teacher who shared with me that a lot of her students aren't good with written English, especially story writing. One of her colleague's scripts was getting so frustrated that he persisted in telling them all how bad they were. Believe me when I say this, their script already tells them, "I'm crap at English" or "I find this difficult". To add insult to injury, their English teacher's script was then confirming to them, yes, you're right, you're terrible at English, in fact "You're so bad, I don't know why I even bother to turn up."

Of course, if you were tuned into Friend FM, you can tell them where or how they could improve, to help them move forward, but please imagine your voice in their heads and how it will sound. "You're a waste of space, you may as well give up" translates in their head to, "I'm a waste of space, I may as well give up" or "You've got the brains of a rocking horse" translates to "I've got the brains of a rocking horse". The latter simply being more pages of negativity, embarrassment, and shame, logged in the pages of their script.

The flipside to this is something more positive like, "The more you focus, the better you'll get". Even if your script is exasperated by their lack of progress, you are installing a new belief that says, "The more I focus the better I'll get" and that can be the first step to changing how they speak to themselves, helping them to tune into Friend FM. Because we human beings always want to prove ourselves right, they will start to find ways to get better using the latter statement.

A good example of this is the fact that I didn't finish reading a whole book until I was about thirty years old. I had started many books, but never actually finished any. I'd fall asleep any time I tried to read, or I'd lose my place and read the same sentences over and over again until I eventually gave up. This finally changed when I started to learn the powerful effects of how we can consciously choose to talk to ourselves and how what you say on the inside has a direct impact on what you experience on the outside.

What you say on the inside has
a direct impact on what you
experience on the outside.

Darren Curtis (Author)

My script went from saying "I hate reading books" or "Reading makes me go to sleep" or "I've never finished a book", which at the time felt true, to consciously saying, "I love reading books" which was definitely not true back then. I would stand in front of the mirror in the morning brushing my teeth, smiling, and repeating my new mantra, "I love reading books". I would laugh to myself, knowing that this was complete and utter bull, but I persisted in my experiment and before long, I found that I seemed to have a book with me wherever I went. I signed up to an evening class where I was required to do a lot of reading about photography and another where I needed to read extensively about hypnotic language patterns. Since then I've read many books on subjects which fascinate me, and I genuinely do now love to read books. Can you see how, by doing this, I turned down the volume on Script FM?

The more positive an identity you can create, the easier your life will be. The easiest way to think of this is every time you say "you" or "you're" when addressing a child, you are potentially adding to that child's identity. So, as I outlined earlier, your "you's" become their "I's". As an example, "You're an idiot" becomes "I'm an idiot" in their head.

> *In the moments of decision,*
> *they will unconsciously hear*
> *your voice in their heads.*
>
> Darren Curtis (Author)

So, it makes me cringe when I work in schools and I hear a teacher's script in the next room verbally destroying a youngster with statements like, "You're a waste of space" or "You stupid little child".

What possible outcome are they looking for when these negative statements are hurled at their students? Surely, they didn't get into teaching because they hated children and wanted to destroy their self-esteem? No, they went into teaching because they wanted to teach, share, and help students to grow. However, teachers have a script, just like you and I, and when that script is triggered, all sorts of abuse will come out of their mouths. The script has effectively hijacked their mouths and is spouting stuff they wouldn't choose to say if they were in control. This is not to say that you can't get annoyed or tell a child off, of course you can, but you must direct your frustrations and annoyance at their behaviour, not their identity.

If you find yourself getting hijacked by your script and you can remain conscious enough, I would suggest you change "You're an idiot" to "You're acting like an idiot" and change "You're irresponsible" to "I will not tolerate your irresponsible behaviour" etc. So, you're still able to let the child know there's a problem and that you're not happy, but you are no longer attacking them as an individual.

What would be even better is to focus on what you want by saying, "I want you to be more responsible" or "Please be sensible and behave", so you're now getting the child to focus on responsibility, being sensible and behaving.

These simple tweaks to your communications will have the effect of avoiding so much trouble in the future.

I was speaking to a nurse who shared a story about her son. She told me how he used to get all the pots and pans out in the kitchen when he was little and he would stand on a stool to mix all sorts of things together to make them fizz and bubble. She went on to tell me how she used to rub his hair and say, "How's my little professor getting on today?"

Today that young child has become one of the youngest people in England to become a professor. I don't know about you, but I don't know too many professors and this chap has not only managed to achieve it but achieved it in less time than normal. I have no doubt that this was assisted by having a mum who gave him the identity of "My little professor" instead of "You messy little git".

So, ask yourself this question: What identities do I give those around me? If you're a parent, what identity are you giving to your child or children?

If you're a teacher, what phrases do you use with your most challenging students?

If it's positive, thank you and well done, you're a great parent/ teacher. If it's negative, I know you haven't been doing it deliberately; like many parents you've probably never realised the effects of attacking a child's identity. But now you do know, with this knowledge comes responsibility, and so I urge you to take the first step and turn those negative "you's" into positive "you's" and see how much easier your life gets when the "challenging" kids start to become what you tell them you'd like them to be.

Playtime

Take a moment now to write down some of the negative phrases you may have used in the past. The more honest you are with yourself now, the more effective this exercise will be.

Negative phrases I have used include...

_____

_____

_____

_____

Positive phrases I could replace them with might be something like ...

_____

_____

_____

_____

_____

We are all Super Heroes, pretending to be ordinary people.

Richard Wilkins

Chapter

nine

Winning the game

Winning the game

An interesting trend I've found in infant and junior schools over the past two decades is the move towards non-competitive sports days. A contradiction in terms, as by its very nature, sports are supposed to be competitive – are they not?

The educational decision-makers claim that taking part in traditional races can be difficult and often embarrassing for many less physically able children.

Never mind the fact that often this is the only area the more physically able youngsters can excel and therefore know what it feels like to be one of the best for a day. To feel like a winner, to show off their physical intelligence and gain the respect of their peers, to be significant.

Always remember the importance
of helping a child to feel significant

Darren Curtis (Author)

My take on this is that many of the decision-makers in education may not have been very good at sport themselves and remember how crap it felt on sports day to be one of the last children to cross the finish line. No matter how hard they tried, they were never going to be recognised with a 2nd or 3rd place medal or rosette, let alone win. In the main, this would have been a very unfamiliar place for them, as the education system suited their way of learning, having been designed by people who learn the same way. They would excel academically and go on to create more examinations and measurements to suit children who prefer to learn like they did, so that the next generation could be like them and excel academically and feel good about themselves. Does that sound likely?

How interesting then that the children who are not academic are constantly measured against criteria which make them feel like a loser every single day. It is made blatantly clear who the clever kids are (measured by current academic standards) and it is the clever kids who are given recognition and positive reinforcement for their achievements, not just by being graded as achieving A*, A and B grades, but by the very fact of having top, middle and bottom sets.

What point am I trying to make? You may well ask.

I remember watching a child at a junior school sports day who was getting very frustrated during an egg and spoon race because, right from the beginning, she was slower than the rest of her classmates. She clearly found it hard to run and balance the egg on the spoon at the same time. No matter how hard she tried, she kept dropping the egg and ended up further and further behind until she got so frustrated, she threw her egg and spoon on the ground. Close to tears, she stormed off the track without finishing. A teacher tried to console her, telling her not to worry, it's OK, not everyone can be good at sport and the fact that it just wasn't her thing. The teacher then went on to comfort her further by reminding her how good she was at other things in the classroom.

Thinking about this story, I commend the teacher for noticing when a child is struggling, for taking the time to make them feel good about themselves and helping to change their perspective on the situation. It's also worth noting that those words, spoken by that teacher on that day, will be adding to that child's positive, encouraging internal voice for years to come. Remember, it is our voice, the words we choose to speak to them as children, that becomes the future internal voice as they grow from a youngster to a teenager and into an adult.

It is a miracle that curiosity survives formal education.

Albert Einstein

My observation that day led me to think about what happens in a similar situation, but one when it is academic performance being judged. Picture a below-average student academically, who just doesn't understand what the teacher is trying to teach in the classroom. No matter how hard they try, they find themselves falling further and further behind, until they eventually get so frustrated, they explode with emotion and often leave the classroom without finishing the lesson.

Does the teacher show the same respect and understanding as to the child who failed to finish the egg and spoon race? Is the child told not to worry, it's OK, not everyone can be good at (insert chosen subject) and the fact that it just isn't their thing and remind them that they're really good at something else? Or does that same teacher's script let the youngster know in no uncertain terms that their behaviour is not acceptable, resulting in the child at best being punished with detention or worse being made to stand alone with no support to stew over how stupid they feel, with their script screaming, "Everybody else gets it, why can't I", "I'm thick, I'm stupid,

I'm dumb", "There's no hope for me", "I hate that bloody teacher", "I hate school", "What's the bloody point" etc, etc.

What's the difference between these two scenarios? We currently live in a society where our children's lives are measured against somebody else's values and criteria of success. How different would it be if children were measured by how confident they are, how healthy they are, how much emotional intelligence they have, how persuasive they are, how effectively they manage money, how easily they find it to create and maintain relationships? In other words, many of the key skills necessary for a long, happy and fulfilling work and personal life.

The original Olympian ideal is held by recognising truth, strength and beauty as well as speed or distance, in this way the qualities of each child are honoured.

Greek Olympian

The theory of multiple intelligences was developed in 1983 by Dr Howard Gardner, professor of education at Harvard University.

It suggests that the traditional notion of intelligence, based on I.Q. testing, is far too limited. Dr Gardner proposes no fewer than eight different intelligences to account for a broader range of human potential in children and adults. These intelligences are:

Linguistic Intelligence ("word smart")
Logical-mathematical Intelligence ("number/reasoning smart")
Spatial Intelligence ("picture smart")
Bodily-Kinaesthetic Intelligence ("body smart")
Musical Intelligence ("music smart")
Interpersonal intelligence ("people smart")
Intrapersonal Intelligence ("self-smart")
Naturalist Intelligence ("nature smart")

Dr Gardner states that our schools and culture focus most of their attention on linguistic and logical-mathematical intelligence. We place high esteem on the highly articulate or logical people in our culture. However, Dr Gardner says that we should also give equal attention to individuals who show gifts in the other intelligences. These are the sorts of people who end up becoming artists, architects, musicians, naturalists, designers, dancers, therapists, entrepreneurs, and others who enrich the world in which we live. However, while our society does recognise the richness of diversity people with these skills bring in adulthood to our lives and our culture, it still continues to suppress and undervalue in childhood and in school the types of intelligence required to be skilled in these ways.

So, many children who have these gifts fail to receive much reinforcement for them in school. Many of these kids, in fact, end up being labelled "Learning disabled", "ADD (Attention Deficit Disorder)", or are simply categorised as under-achievers. And yet, they often display unique and valuable ways of thinking and learning which just don't happen to fit neatly in a heavily linguistic or logical-mathematical classroom.

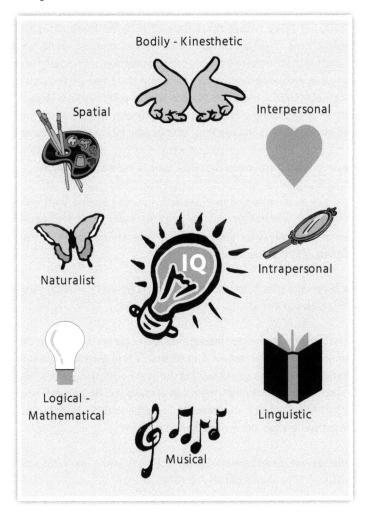

The theory of multiple intelligences proposes a major transformation in the way our schools are run. It suggests that teachers be trained to present their lessons in a wide variety of ways, using music, cooperative learning, art activities, role play, multimedia, field trips, inner reflection, and much more.

The good news is that the theory of multiple intelligences has grabbed the attention of many educators around the world, and hundreds of schools are currently using its philosophy to redesign the way they educate children. The bad news is that there are thousands of schools still out there that teach in the same old dull way, through dry lectures, boring worksheets, and textbooks. The challenge is to enlighten many more teachers, school administrators, and others who work with children, so that each child has the opportunity to learn in ways harmonious with their specific type of intelligence.

Our job as parents and teachers is to recognise what each child is good at and nurture it. We need to make them feel better about themselves by acknowledging their strengths rather than highlighting their weaknesses.

Rob Parsons puts it so well in his book *TEENAGERS – What Every Parent Has to Know*:[1]

"Imagine the scene: our teenage daughter comes home with her school report. She's got an A in History, a B in Maths, and a D in French. What do we spend most of the next hour talking about? The French of course? We say, "How can we help you do better in your French? Shall we get you some study guides in GCSE French? How about some audio tapes or perhaps a tutor?

Where's the parent who will say, 'Let's get you a tutor for your History!" "But, Mum, I got an A in History!"

---

1   Hodder & Stoughton, 2007

"I know. Let's make you even better at what you're already good at."

I understand the need to get a spread of GCSEs – and the pressure therefore of trying to keep all the plates in the air – but especially with the seemingly less able child, it's vital to send them into life knowing that they have found at least one strength and that they have a parent who is helping them to develop it."

> *Let them know you love them*
> *irrespective of their achievements.*

Rob Parsons – Author

Playtime

What is your child really good at?

_____

_____

_____

_____

Where do they display natural talent?

_____

_____

_____

_____

What can you do to encourage their natural talent?

_____

_____

_____

_____

Chapter

ten

Pick your battles

Pick your battles

When you transfer your script's frustration, upset and anger from one battle to the next, to the next, you will find you are fighting a series of losing battles. In the past you may have found your script stacking past negative events and then reminding you of those events every time it witnesses anything it perceives to be similar, which only serves to trigger more negative emotions and builds up a barrier of resentment. Unfortunately, resentment only leads to blame and blame doesn't help you or your child. And while your script is busy blaming others it blinds you to the many options you have available to you.

The common battles I come across create a familiar list: the untidy room battle, the doing your homework at the last minute battle, the coming home late battle, the spending too much time on the games console battle, the talking with your mouth full battle, the not pulling your weight around the house battle... insert your favourite battle here battle!! The list goes on.

The problem is, your script is probably moaning as much about the trivial things as it is about the more serious things. This results in the punishment or severity of the moaning not necessarily fitting the crime. This will often mean that your script's criticism not only comes across as unfair but IS unfair and inconsistent. Worse than that, as we mentioned in the Values chapter, if you have a child who places a high value on fairness, their script's reaction to any feeling of injustice or unfairness will be extreme. The more battles your script is trying to win the more stacked emotion your script will have stored and therefore the more challenging your script will find it to let go, especially if your script places a high value on control. Can you see why it is so important to understand that you are not your script? This last paragraph serves to emphasise how you get hijacked by your script on a daily basis.

When you break down how much time your script spends moaning, nagging or being stressed, stand back and analyse all the battles your script is fighting. Based on the evidence of thousands of parents I have spoken to about this, I would estimate that 80% of your emotional strength is being used up on just one ongoing battle and the remaining 20% is used up on the rest. Do you recognise this in your battles? It therefore makes sense to focus your energy into fixing the one battle which is causing you the most grief.

If you could only win one battle, what's the most important one for you to win?

Remember the story from the first chapter, where the mum was getting annoyed about so many different things, but when she chose to focus her efforts on the main battle she would like to win, the battle that caused 80% of the arguments in her home, I was able to help her to find a solution.

If you're sharing your life with teens or pre-teens, right now they are going through a scary set of emotional and physical changes. So, if you can learn to focus on the thing that will give you the greatest result for the least amount of effort, I would suggest you aim to solve that one thing. After all, it can be tiring for you and for them if your script is constantly trying to get everyone to do everything you want.

*Live through deeds of love, and
let others live with tolerance
for their unique intentions.*

Rudolf Steiner

The following may help with your perception behind some of your battles:

With every action or communication, we have an intention. The person or people at the receiving end of our action or communication will interpret what we mean. Depending on the interpretation they give it, there will be a resulting impact.

I call this the three 'i' triangle.

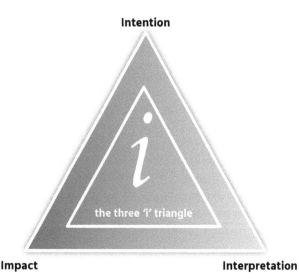

Intention

i

the three 'i' triangle

Impact   **Interpretation**

Let's imagine you ask your child to tidy their room. Your intention is to restore some order so that you can feel more relaxed. Their interpretation is that you're nagging, so your child doesn't clean their room. At this point, things escalate. Their intention is to relax but your interpretation is that they are being disrespectful. The impact is that your script gets annoyed and you find yourself shouting at them, they then shout back, and the whole thing descends into a full-blown argument. Your script is arguing with their script!

> *Two people's scripts cause an argument; two countries' scripts cause a war.*
>
> Richard Wilkins

Which is interesting, because both of your intentions were the same, but when your script interacts with someone else's script everyone misinterprets what the other meant. When you communicate from a place of kindness and calm, which is how you would always choose to communicate, you would never have another argument again. Unfortunately, even when you know about the script, you will still get hijacked by your script and still get sucked into disagreements and arguments, but the arguments will not last as long, and it will be so much easier to say sorry once all your senses return.

When you ask if they need to do some homework, your intention is to be helpful, to merely prompt and remind them to do something they are required to do. Their script's interpretation is that you're interfering or nagging them just for the sake of it, so they ignore you. Their intention at this point is to be left alone but your script interprets this as rude. The impact of this is to annoy you, which escalates into an argument, resulting in the final impact of you both being annoyed and the homework being even less likely to be done than if it had never been mentioned.

If you could have held on to your original intention of being helpful and understand how their script had misinterpreted what you meant, you could have continued trying to be helpful or maybe the biggest help could have been to have left them alone, which is what they wanted, and let them face the consequence of not doing their homework. Learning the lesson of consequence will help their roots to grow, it challenges them to be more independent, to not have to rely on you so much. Ponder this point about reliance. Do you in fact want them to rely on you, because your script likes to feel needed, even though your script moans about it? These are the sorts of paradoxes our script will get us into from time to time!

I remember chatting to a colleague who felt her son was spending too much time on his games console in his bedroom. She was really concerned that at sixteen years old he was spending hours on end in his room with his mates and their world seemed to revolve around these senseless games (her script's words not mine). Does this sound familiar? When I asked what her main concern was, she said she felt he should be spending more time playing outside and less time wasting his life in his bedroom.

I remember sharing with her a story about a parent whose main battle was getting her fifteen-year-old son to come home at night. He would often stay out into the early hours of the morning, getting drunk or smoking green leafy substances.

My colleague looked at me in sheer horror saying, "Oh my god, I'm so lucky to know where my son is every night, he's such a good lad, he does really well at school and he has a really good group of friends. Him spending time in his room seems quite insignificant now doesn't it? I'm going to go home and give him a hug and tell him how much I appreciate him."

We all do it don't we? We get so wrapped up in what seems like a battle, when it's completely trivial in the grand scheme of things.

It's often something our script has blown up out of all proportion, but we only realise this when something or someone places our situation with our own children back into perspective. This then allows us to appreciate all the good things about them and to see our own ability to be good parents.

When I was a boy and I wanted to learn to swim, I tried my hardest to thrash about in the water, but the harder I tried, the quicker I sank. I thought to myself, what would happen if I tried to do the opposite? So, I completely relaxed, I trusted in the situation and I just let go. Hey presto! I could float. This is something I keep reminding myself in life: when I remember to relax, trust, and let go, I float.

Darren Curtis (Author)

Playtime

What three areas would you be willing to relax, trust and let go of?

1._____

2._____

3._____

Chapter

eleven

Listening

Listening

I'm sure you'll agree that the greatest gift you can give to anyone is that of your attention, and the best form of attention is to listen. When a child wants to talk, listen. It may not always be the most interesting of conversations, but they have chosen to chat to you about what is important to them at that moment in time. By paying them the courtesy of stopping what you are doing and listening, you are sending them a clear message: "You're important to me" and "You are significant". Kids who grow up feeling important and significant don't need to seek it elsewhere later in life by joining gangs or taking drugs, especially during the teenage years.

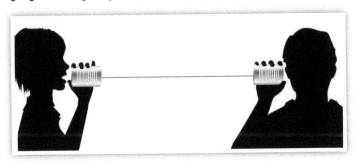

When I've asked teenagers what they want from their parents, they will reply, "I want my parents to feel I'm someone special". Let them know they are special to you. Remember Craig and what he was willing to do to make his mum proud?

"I want my parents to be warm and friendly to me, just like when they answer the door or the phone". Isn't it funny how we often keep our most focused listening for strangers and treat the people we love with the most disregard?

Consider this: a child who is used to being told to shut up or told to come back later because you're too busy (a slightly more polite way of saying shut up) will eventually stop bothering to communicate.

So, don't be surprised when they become a teenager who just grunts at you most of the time, exercising their new-found freedom to do as they wish. This is because somewhere on their script, their negative internal voice will be saying, "They never listen to me, so why should I bother talking to them?" We all have a need to be listened to and if they don't feel listened to by you, who are they finding to listen to them? Whoever that is that they turn to now has a significant influence over your child. Depending on who that is, that person could have a positive influence on them, but there is also a chance that influence could be negative. If you invest in listening early on, as they grow you will reap the rewards, as it will be you they turn to for advice and guidance instead of the person you have no control over.

There are three kinds of listening. There is the conversational style of listening, often referred to as the '*Me* Too' method of listening. This is what we all commonly employ for day-to-day interactions with people.

In 'Me Too' mode, someone says something and while they are talking you are listening, but you are also relating the subject to something in your life, so that you can answer when they stop talking. The amount of information you hear will depend on how interested you were in the person or subject.

The second kind of listening is *active* listening. This is where your mind is empty, and you have no pre-conceived ideas or judgement. You are really listening to what the person is saying, allowing them the time and space to express themselves. Your only interest is in them; you are not interested in yourself. This type of listening takes some practice, but it is an extremely useful way to build strong relationships, especially with your partner and your children.

Thirdly, there is *dynamic* listening. This is where you are listening to what is NOT being said; you are interpreting what is going on behind a conversation. This is listening in its highest form and it requires skill and even training to master this successfully. Many professions require people to be skilled at dynamic listening, to the point where they can be considered what I call 'professional listeners'. I would include psychologists, counsellors, and coaches in this list of professions. Of course, some are better at this than others! Crucially though, two other groups of people should aim to become professional listeners: teachers and parents. By doing so, we can pass on the skill of listening to the most important group of all, our children, or the children we are teaching.

I often hear parents and teachers telling children they need to learn to listen, but where exactly should they learn this skill from? Listening is generally not taught in schools, or even considered an area to be taught. In turn, the majority of teachers I know find it extremely hard to listen because their job is primarily not to listen but to teach, which involves speaking and imparting information.

Like most skills, listening is one that takes some practice and I would suggest we all need to learn to listen more. A great way to teach a child to listen is to sit down with them one-to-one and ask some open questions and listen to their reply.

Try asking these questions:

What's your favourite thing to do?
What is it about that specific thing that you enjoy?
What's your favourite memory?
What is it about that specific memory that you like?
What do you wish we could do more of?

Please note: If they ever say, "I don't know", say "If you did know the answer, what would it be?" If they really don't know, just leave it, and go on to the next question. It's just a bit of fun.

Give them time to answer. If they don't answer immediately, allow them a bit of silence to think if necessary. Silence is a good thing; it means they are thinking about their reply.

Remember, the purpose of the exercise is for you to properly listen, with no pre-conceived ideas, no judgement, no right or wrong, no adding in what you think. You are giving them the time and space to express themselves and by doing so you will find out a bit more about your child. You may be surprised what you learn when you just shut up and listen.

You will also be leading by example. You will be teaching your child how to listen and demonstrating that you care enough to ask questions *and* to listen to the answers.

Proper listening will also help to avoid so many arguments, as often it's the absence of proper listening which causes the misunderstanding or misinterpretation in the first place. Look back to the three 'i' triangle in Chapter 9 to underline the importance of this.

If you spend ten extra seconds listening, you may save yourself ten minutes of arguing and possibly ten years of regret about words you didn't mean to say, all because you bothered to listen.

Some personality types are more emotional in their responses than others, but I'm sure you'll agree that, as a rule, teenagers love to respond with emotion. This is OK, it's normal. Think of all your best memories from childhood. Events such as parties, Christmas, and holidays all have emotions attached to them. Emotions are good!

Creating an environment which is conducive to talking makes such a difference, which is why eating together as a family is so important. I take each of my boys away every year, just me and one of them for at least a long weekend. We use this time and space to chat, share stories and chill out. It allows us to spend uninterrupted time together on a one-to-one basis while the other one stays at home with his mum where they too get some quality one-to-one time together.

Encourage them to get out and about, to do things with you from an early age so it becomes a habit. You will then reap the benefits as you grow together. If they have cultivated an interest or a hobby, it's important that you show an interest, even if it's not strictly your thing.

Your relationship with your children is like an emotional bank account that you are either adding to or taking away from. If you don't ensure that your emotional bank account stays in credit, the costs can start to build up in the form of their performance at school, poor behaviour, poor choice of friends, desire to spend less and less time with you... the list is endless.

When it comes to your kids the amount of time and effort you put in with them today will pay dividends as they get older. If you listen to them, they will return the favour later by listening to you and the advice you give and responding to your requests. You will have taught them *by example*. If you take the time to sit down and talk, you will have established a communications channel they have become familiar with using and one they trust works. If the script wants to fool you that you are too busy and need to regularly work late, you are sending them a clear signal that "My work is more important than you." Of all the regrets I hear parents express as their children grow older, not spending enough time with them when they were younger is the most common one. The problem is that at that point you cannot fix it. When that time has gone, it's gone. You may have a healthy bank balance and feel important at work, but you'll feel terrible when you wake up one morning and realise you are no longer important to the people who matter more, your son or daughter.

Playtime

When do you intend to sit down and give them a good listening to?

Date:_____

What three things did you learn from that conversation?

1._____

_____

2._____

_____

3._____

_____

If you don't listen eagerly to the little stuff when they are little, they won't tell you the big stuff when they are big, because to them all of it has always been big stuff.

Catherine M. Wallace

Chapter

twelve

Perception is reality

Perception is reality

Picture the scene: a pair of 1930s semi-detached homes, blackened broken windows and charred window frames, most of the roof missing, except for some charcoal smouldering woodwork which used to hold the roof and roof tiles in position, both homes completely destroyed by fire. The fire engines are still spraying water onto the roof to ensure no secondary fires start, but it is clear that everything inside both homes has been burnt to a cinder. A man is sitting on the curb outside the house on the left with his head in his hands; his wife and children, although clearly distressed, are trying to comfort him. He looks extremely angry and you overhear him commenting to them, "This is the last bloody straw, why does this crap always happen to us? As if life isn't bad enough already. What have we done to deserve this? We've lost everything, I must be the unluckiest man in the world".

You turn to see a car pull up outside the house on the right. A man jumps out and runs to his wife and children who are standing by the fire engine, with the biggest smile on his face. He throws his arms around them and declares, "Thank god, you're all OK, it's only stuff, we can replace all the stuff, I love you all so much, I am truly the luckiest man in the world". The event is the same for both parents, but their perceptions are worlds apart. Can you see that the first man has clearly been hijacked by his script, which always focuses on fear and lack, whereas the other man is not in his script and is coming from a place of love and gratitude. It's worth noting here that you cannot be fearful and grateful at the same time; you're either in the script or you're being your authentic self.

Ever noticed how, when something happens in a teenager's life, they exaggerate the story and blow it up to be something much more than it really is? Does this annoy your script? Which one of your values does this dishonour? Maybe honesty? But if you know that most teenagers are going to exaggerate, why not just let them, but view it from a different angle, change your perception. Maybe their intention is to make the story more interesting. Maybe their intention is to be more significant in the story or to you. If you can change your perception of your teenager's behaviour, then a positive change in your reaction to that behaviour will automatically follow.

The power of a positively framed question

Your brain loves to answer the questions you pose to yourself. If your script poses a negative question, your brain will usually reply with an equally negative answer. As we have mentioned previously, this is your script trying to prove itself right.

Here is an example of a negative question in your head: "Why do they always answer me back?"

A possible negative answer would be, "Because they don't respect me." Another negative question: "Why won't they do as they're told?" Possible negative answer: "Because they're trying to annoy me."

Let us look at how much better it is to ask yourself a positively framed question which will allow your brain to work on a positive solution. Another good technique is to change the frequency from Script FM to Friend FM again.

Positive question: "What can I do to gain more respect?"

Possible positive answer: "Be consistent, have more self-respect and ask for what I want."

Positive question: "What needs to happen to encourage people to listen to me?"

Possible positive answer: "Stay calm and lead by example."

If you feel that life has become a bit too serious, allow yourself to lighten up and laugh a little more. It's easier to think of positive questions to ask yourself when you have a smile on your face.

The magic of metaphor

If you hear yourself saying things like, "Being a parent is an uphill struggle" or "I seem to be taking two steps forwards and one step back", your script is not only building a vivid picture of the problem, it now has emotion linked to it as it says to itself, "Here's a statement, it's a fact, let's go and find some more evidence to prove ourselves right." To underline this point, please refer back to Chapter One and Chapter Six.

It is far more useful to eliminate any negative metaphors and replace them with brighter, more positive images for the brain to work on. It is better for you to choose your own so that this becomes something personal and unique to you. However, to give you an idea, something like, "Being a parent is a wonderful journey" or "I seem to be progressing in leaps and bounds" would be the positive alternatives to the previous negative metaphors. By choosing these positive alternatives, your brain now says, "Ok, we've got new statements and images to work with, let's go and find some new evidence to prove ourselves right."

Your script may be saying to you at this point, "No Darren, my brain is saying, that's a lie, I don't believe being a parent is a wonderful journey and I don't seem to be progressing in leaps and bounds." I respect that, but we need to loosen the grip of the script's old metaphors which are no longer serving you or your family. Also, I presume that by reading this far you're open to trying something a little different to help you to get a favourable end-result. Remember the fly at the window in Chapter One...

Playtime

Answer the following questions, coming up with at least four options for each question.

What can I do to help make my life as a parent a wonderful journey?

1._____

2._____

3._____

4._____

What can I do to help myself progress in leaps and bounds?

1._____

2._____

3._____

4._____

Draw a picture of your new metaphor. Just a basic picture is fine, relax and let go, use colour, the more child-like the better.

Past examples from parents have been: "Life is like a bowl of cherries."

"Communicating with my children is as easy as shelling peas."

And finally, go and buy yourself a postcard, fridge magnet or picture which represents your new metaphor.

People often ask me if I'm aiming for some kind of unrealistic utopia for families. I find this ironic, as in many ways I am aiming at the reverse of this. My aim is to instil confidence in parents (and children) and this is usually created through a process of adversity and struggle. Some of the most interesting people I know would not have the strength of character they have today without the challenges they were presented with in their formative years. By emerging from the fire of conflict intact, parents and children are stronger, and so is their relationship.

The years leading up to being a teenager and throughout the teenage years are critical as a rite of passage for children. They are learning so many life lessons and are in unfamiliar territory, often resulting in conflict at home or in school. So, my main aim is for our children to grow into happy, healthy, confident adults, able to make good choices, cope with the challenges life will throw their way and for them to fulfil their potential. After all, it is the trees which grow in stormy, windy climates where the weather challenges then to grow stronger, thicker, deeper roots which are able to stay upright.

> *What happens to a man is*
> *less significant than what*
> *happens within him.*
>
> Louis L. Mann

When you allow yourself to view a child from a completely different perspective, you will also be allowing your relationship to change for the better.

Remember, I've been sharing with you how we or our script consistently tries to prove things to us depending on the beliefs we hold about a certain person, situation or ourselves. If you believe little Johnny is an attention seeking pain in the arse, you'll find every shred of evidence to support your script's negative belief.

If you can find it in yourself to believe that little Johnny is trying his best and appreciate Johnny has other qualities which you are committed to uncovering, you will find you are calmer and more forgiving of the things that used to wind your script up about him.

This is why you have to be so careful if you have favourites. Favouritism can be just as damaging for the child who is the favourite as well as the child who is not.

The *Harry Potter* films beautifully illustrate to us the downside of favouritism, as we all root for Harry against his spoilt cousin Dudley Dursley. You can see how Harry can never get anything right in his aunt and uncle's eyes and Dudley can never get anything wrong. Harry does everything to try to please them in the beginning, but as their scripts always find fault, eventually Harry gives up trying. On the other hand, Dudley is not allowed to grow as an individual because his mother and father's scripts are constantly doing everything for him.

Let them know that they are loved unconditionally; that they are safe, and they belong, but also challenge them often to take on things outside of their comfort zone. This will build resilience and independence and a feeling of significance. It will be a crucial part of the process of increasing their confidence.

We *all* crave significance in some way and if a child can't find a way to achieve this in a positive way, they will achieve it in a negative way.

A child that hits another child is significant to the other child in that moment.

A teenager who smokes a cigarette or takes a drug wants to show off, act older or belong. Showing off, acting older and a desire to belong are all ways of expressing a yearning for significance or connection.

A youngster who becomes the leader of a gang has gained the significance they crave. The teenager who carries a knife or a gun gains a forced respect/fear from their peers and therefore also has fulfilled their need for significance.

You would think that throwing a child in at the deep end would toughen them up, wouldn't you? And calling them a wimp because they can't or won't do it, would make them more confident, wouldn't it?

No, no, no, of course not. It is more likely to have the opposite effect to building confidence and significance and lead to anxiety, uncertainty, self-doubt and making them feel like a failure.

Try some simple things, like encouraging your child when they're younger to take items back to the shop and allowing them to ask the shop assistant or cashier if they can exchange things, or ordering their own food in a cafe or restaurant, instead of relying on you to do it for them. All of this will help them to become better and more confident communicators and to feel more significant in a positive way.

Playtime

Encouragement and support are the key, so answer yourself these simple questions:

What things would I like to change right now?

_____

_____

_____

What would I like to start doing?

_____

_____

_____

What would I like to stop doing?

_____

_____

_____

*Give your child the roots to
grow and the wings to fly.*

Jim Rohn

Chapter

thirteen

Eat, drink and be happy...

Eat, drink and be happy...

Some parents hire me to work with their children when they have been diagnosed with Attention Deficit Hyperactivity Disorder (ADHD), anger management or behavioural issues. I start by asking them who diagnosed the condition. The reply is usually a doctor, who has often issued a prescription as part of the consultation. My next question is, "What did they say about diet?"

"Nothing," is usually the reply.

How can any responsible medical professional prescribe drugs with serious side-effects to a child without finding out to begin with what they are consuming on a regular basis?

Starting where I believe the doctors should have started, I ask the youngster to write down everything they've eaten and drank in the last twenty-four hours. The following is a list I received from a recent client:

7:00am   Cereal and milk (one of the main ingredients of the cereal was sugar)

8:00am   Chocolate bar and can of coke on the way to school (main ingredients: sugar and caffeine)

10:20am   Energy drink (main ingredients: sugar and caffeine)

1:00pm   Hot dog, chips, and energy drink (high fat, high sugar, caffeine)

3:20pm   Crisps and can of coke on the way home from school (high fat, high sugar, caffeine)

3:45pm   Biscuits and crisps (high fat, high sugar)

5:00pm   Cheese and tomato pizza and chips and can of coke (high fat, high sugar, high caffeine)

6:30pm   Energy drink (high sugar and high caffeine)

8:00pm   Cereal and milk (high sugar)

If one of my boys consumed even half that diet for just one day, I wouldn't want to be in the same room as him. He'd be rude, restless, obnoxious, annoying, answering me back; the list of negative behaviour would be endless. We would argue, and the sad thing is, it wouldn't be *his* fault; I'd be arguing with a dehydrated, sugar and caffeine-fuelled lunatic.

This child is not suffering from ADHD. They are consuming far too much sugar, caffeine and processed food and not enough still water, fruit and vegetables.

Go back to basics

If you go back to basics, healthy food and drink will help you and your child to be calmer and happier. What they eat is a habit, and it is up to you to help them to change any unhealthy eating habits. I'm conscious that it is likely that unhealthy eating habits are usually inherited and learned from adults. So, if you're serious about helping your child to have better moods and behaviour, may I be so bold as to suggest you take ownership of what you eat as a family. If you are not eating enough healthy food (e.g. fruit, vegetables and non-processed foods) and drinking enough still water, then you need to make the necessary changes to start introducing these foods.

The water content of the average healthy person is a surprising 60%. Interestingly, in someone who is obese this reduces to 45%. It's worth noting that we often get confused between the signal from the brain to let us know we are thirsty and interpret this instead as a signal that we are hungry. This means we eat when we should be drinking water. A great tip here is to drink a glass of water each time you feel hungry and wait for ten minutes. If you still feel hungry, then it's time to eat.

The majority of our brain is comprised of water and when fully hydrated we gain clarity of thought, we find it easier to concentrate and this has a positive effect on our mood. In fact, dehydration is a significant cause of headaches and with a headache we are invariably far less tolerant of negative behaviour. Is that because our children's behaviour became worse? No, it is our level of tolerance which has dropped. Just by making minor tweaks to your diet and being conscious of the type and amount of fluid you and/or your child consumes, you can control the number of headaches you get and therefore improve your coping and tolerance levels.

A really simple way to know that you and your child are taking in a minimum quota of water is to buy or fill a 2-litre bottle of water and take regular sips throughout the day, with the aim of consuming all the water by the end of the day. In my experience this one simple tweak to your routines will lead to a significant improvement in yours and your teenager's general mood and tolerance levels.

It is so important to consume fruits and vegetables which contain the trace minerals, vitamins and anti-oxidants we so vitally need to maintain our health and which help to regulate our moods even further. By adding these things into yours and your child's diet you will find you are calmer and more able to cope with the day-to-day challenges which occur, especially when teenagers are involved.

After visiting a nutritionist, I found I was lacking in zinc and magnesium. After seeking out foods which were higher in these minerals and taking a good quality "true food" mineral supplement every day, I found my mood improved significantly. If I'm easily stressed or agitated these days my kids joke, "Have you taken your minerals today Dad". So, it's worth getting yours or your child's mineral levels checked by a professional nutritionist prior to going down the prescribed drugs route.

Playtime

What have I eaten and drunk in the last 24 hours?

_____

_____

_____

What has my child eaten and drunk in the last 24 hours?

_____

_____

_____

What three small changes am I going to make to help improve my tolerance levels?

_____

_____

_____

Chapter

fourteen

Keep calm and carry on...

Keep calm and carry on...

I'm always interested in how you know if you're having a good day or a bad day. What emotions are you experiencing which let you know you're having a good day? Happiness, calm, excitement, joy, peace, harmony – choose or add the words which resonate with you.

On a bad day you may be feeling anger, annoyance, irritation, upset, guilt, depression, jealousy, fear, confusion – again, choose or add the words which resonate with you.

All the positive emotions put us in a resourceful state, where we can connect with our children and get the best from them. The negative emotions create an unresourceful state where our script will say things we regret, attack, blame and bring out the worst in our children.

Although it can be common to have a completely good day or a completely bad day, I'm sure you'll agree, you and I will generally experience a range of emotions throughout a given day or week.

We can be going along merrily, feeling positive emotions but then suddenly someone or something happens which makes us flip to negative emotions. I like to refer to these as *triggers*. If somebody says something to annoy you, how your script has interpreted what they said was the trigger. If you suddenly feel overwhelmed, the last thing you took on was the trigger.

We all have different triggers depending on our values and beliefs, so something which will be annoying to your script may well slip past somebody else's without being noticed. It's worth thinking back to the story of the youngsters in the alleyway and the perceived disrespect in Chapter Four.

Similarly, if your child does something to make you feel proud, and you've taken the time to notice, it can easily take you in an instant from feeling a negative emotion (being in your script) to a positive emotion of sheer joy. Something as simple as someone showing you some appreciation may help you go from being annoyed to feeling happy or, dare I say, *appreciated*. But once again, the trick is to notice when you're being appreciated, and this may involve changing any negative beliefs your script may hold regarding how appreciated you currently feel.

But we don't have to be dependent on others to change our emotions. The most important thing to realise is that we all have our own triggers for helping us to go from an unresourceful state to a resourceful state. You may choose to read a book, relax in a hot bath, or go for a walk to calm down, as it is often the simplest of pleasures which help us to relax. Funnily enough, the only thing usually stopping you from doing these things is your script or your script's belief around your ability to do them.

During the safety briefing on a plane, why does the airline representative tell you, "In the event of the cabin losing air pressure, when the oxygen masks drop, please ensure you fit your own oxygen mask before you attempt to fit your child's oxygen mask"?

If you run out of oxygen, you won't be able to help your child. We can only give our children what they need when our own needs have been met.

> *Take rest; a field that has rested gives a bountiful crop.*
>
> Ovid

It's often so easy to forget how easy it is to get back to a resourceful state, a state where we can help ourselves and others. We often ignore the opportunities around us by listening to our script telling us we're too busy. Once again I'd like to remind you of the power of your words and thoughts and if you continue to listen to your script telling you how busy you are, you will continue to create busyness.

A more useful mantra to adopt would be something like, "I constantly surprise myself how much I am able to achieve each day" or "I always seem to find time to relax and have fun." It's a new instruction for your brain to work on and it will help you to come up with the most wonderful and unexpected solutions to prove you right.

The calmer and nicer you are to yourself and to your kids, the calmer and nicer they'll be to you – remember the hall of a thousand mirrors in Chapter 4?

If you're committed to taking responsibility for yours and your family's long-term emotional stability, one of the easiest things you can do is start with the things which you have the most control over. I trust you have started to realise you have so much more control over your own thoughts and actions than you do over other people's. So, when you choose to change, to go beyond your script, the way you think and act, the situations and people around you will start to change for the better. With this new empowerment, I would suggest you choose to make a commitment to yourself today to deliberately and consciously start to gain and maintain a healthy work/life balance, because with balance you reach a resourceful state more easily and more often.

However, before we continue, may I ask, are you the type of person who keeps a promise?

Great, I knew you were, because in the next exercise I want you to make six promises to yourself which will have the greatest positive effect on your relationship with your children.

Just remember to focus on what you want and make it as specific as possible. An example of this would be, "I promise to sit down and have a family meal together at least five times per week", which is more useful than "I promise to eat fewer takeaways" – you get the gist.

I promise

_____

I promise

_____

I promise

_____

I promise

_____

I promise

_____

I promise...

_____

Now I would guess that each promise will require some action to be taken. So, depending on your personality type, you may wish to break down each action into smaller steps. For example, if one of your promises is to drink two litres of still water per day, your first step may be to buy a 2-litre water container or to buy a week's supply of still spring water from your local supermarket.

Please answer the following question:

My first step for reaching each of my promises is to:

1. _____

2. _____

3. _____

4. _____

5. _____

6. _____

I'm sure you'll agree how important these promises are to enable you to focus on what you want, instead of what you don't want. They will also help pull you towards what it is you want, instead of trying to push yourself. Pushing takes effort, being pulled towards your goal is so much easier.

I'm a recovering procrastinator, so I know from experience how hard it can sometimes be to stay focused. I've even been compared to a magpie, who keeps getting distracted by the shiny things around me which have absolutely nothing to do with my main goals in life.

So, we need to ensure your goals are so compelling you will be naturally drawn towards them.

One thing that really helped me was an interview I heard with Sir Matthew Pinsent, the British Olympic rower. He was asked about the fourth gold medal he'd won as part of the four-man rowing team at Athens in 2004 and how they'd achieved it considering their poor performance at the World Championships the previous year. He explained that the team had got together after the poor results and asked themselves openly and honestly if they really wanted to win Olympic gold medals the following year and if they did, were they prepared to do whatever it took to reach that goal?

Agreeing that they all did want it to happen, they recognised the fact that they were a four-man rowing team, a manager, physiotherapists, trainers, nutritionists, sponsors, boat builders and supporters, all putting forward different opinions and ideas. There was a lot of well-meaning input from various sources. Sometimes, however, this input was contradictory, which resulted in a negative effect on their ability to stay focused. So, they developed a simple strategy to help them to *make decisions*.

The strategy was in the form of a question. As you know, if you ask yourself great questions, you get great answers. The question they chose was, "Will it make the boat go faster?" Simple but fantastically effective. Just imagine for one minute your goal is to win a gold medal at the Olympics and with every decision you make from that moment on, you ask yourself, "Will this make the boat go faster?" Should I go to the pub tonight? Should I have a glass of wine with my lunch? Should I miss training today? Should I ask for more support? Should I go to bed early tonight? Should I eat this chocolate cake?

Well, here's a thing you may not be aware of, we all have a primary question that we ask ourselves unconsciously all the time.

So, what question do you need to create to help you stay focused on your goal? Or which question could you suggest which would help a child to stay focused?

If you're a parent with a goal to spend more quality time with your children, you may want to ask yourself the question, "What will help me spend more quality time with my children?" or "Will this help me spend more quality time with my children?" Thinking about this in practice, when a friend invites you to have a drink after work for the third time this week, I would imagine your answer would be different if you asked the question first: "Will this help me spend more quality time with my children?" Or when you're asked if you can help a colleague on a new committee or project, "Will this help me spend more quality time with my children?" It's your shout...

If you're a teacher who decides you want to go all-out to help make learning more enjoyable for your students, you may choose to ask, "How can I get the learning across to my students in a fun way?" or "Will this help to engage my students?" I guarantee you'll be more creative in your lesson planning.

Remember, whatever questions you habitually ask yourself will keep getting answered. This is what some of the greatest minds in history have done. They habitually asked themselves a positive question, until they come up with the answer.

Ask yourself great questions and encourage your children to do the same, helping you both to shift from becoming problem solvers to solution seekers.

The pupil with a new desire to pass a certain exam might ask, "What can I do to improve my English grades?"

For Craig, who realises that his goal in life is to make his mum proud, he would only need to ask, "Will this make my mum proud?" So, when his friends start smoking and offer him a cigarette, instead of asking, "Will this help me to look older?" or "Will this help me to fit in?", he'll ask himself "Will this make my mum proud?" You and I now know the answer to that internal question and that the outcome will be totally different, don't we?

Playtime:

What are your 3 biggest takeaways from reading this book and completing the questions?

1. _____

_____

_____

2. _____

_____

_____

3. _____

_____

_____

Congratulations on completing The Awakened Parent Challenge. I honour your commitment.

If you haven't completed the online challenge, there's still time, simply pop over to www.darrencurtis.com/challenge.

*Today will never
come again
Be a blessing
Be a friend
Encourage someone
Take time to care
Let your words heal,
and not wound.*

Unknown

Lightning Source UK Ltd.
Milton Keynes UK
UKHW020800231020
372092UK00005B/211